CAMPUS
renewal

A **PRACTICAL** PLAN

FOR **UNITING CAMPUS MINISTRIES**

IN **PRAYER** & **MISSION**

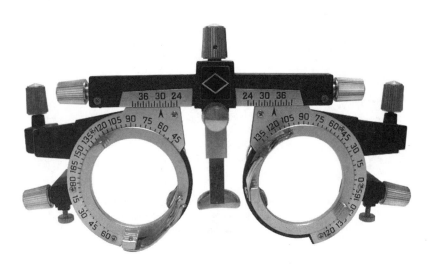

Justin Christopher

Campus Renewal
A Practical Plan for Uniting Campus
Ministries in Prayer and Mission
Justin Christopher

Campus Renewal Ministries
2421 #B San Antonio St.
Austin, TX 78705

(512) 331-5991 | www.campusrenewal.org

ORDERING INFORMATION
To order additional copies, call (512) 331-5991 or visit
www.campusrenewal.org.

CREDITS
Copyeditor: Deborah Costenbader
Designer: Joel Skotak, Sko Design Lab

Endorsements

"I have known and worked with Justin for almost two decades. He was actively working toward building united prayer-based missional movements long before these concepts became more mainstream. This book is not just full of good ideas or general theological statements. Instead, everything in it comes from tested principles, which have been worked out in a real-life environment — namely the University of Texas. If you are interested in seeing the Church gain better leverage to transform a city, campus, or country, then this is the book for you."

Jeremy Story
President, Campus Renewal Ministries

"*Campus Renewal* is a chronicle of hope. It provides the story of a profound movement of God that is underway; but it also builds on-ramps for others who want to merge into this stream. I am hoping that the lessons here will be adopted by church leaders everywhere and applied to their ministry settings. If that happens, then the story of what is happening at the University of Texas could become your story too."

Reggie McNeal
Missional Leadership Specialist, Leadership Network, Dallas ,Texas

"Wow. What a powerful story of transformation and seeing God turn a campus 'right-side up'! Could this kind of spiritual teamwork, revival, and impact happen at your school? Read, enjoy, soak it in, then ask the Lord to use you to spark a prayer-saturated, Christ-exalting, Body-unifying movement at your college."

Steve Shadrach
Founder, Student Mobilization and author of Fuel and the Flame

"Justin tells it well. You can sense right away that you aren't being sold on a program, but instead, you're being told a true story. Justin unfolds the true story in a way that highlights the truths that he and others have lived and learned over many years. I've known and walked (literally) with Justin and others at UT for years. I doubt you'll be able to read this story and fail to be encouraged to keep pressing on in prayer-sustained biblical hope for your campus or community."

STEVE HAWTHORNE
Co-editor of Perspectives on the World Christian Movement

"Are you a campus minister or a Christian student looking for practical input on how to transform your campus? Are you looking for something that is Kingdom-minded, Spirit-led, and will help you find the way forward even amidst a challenging situation? If so, you are holding in your hands a treasure of wisdom that will help you see your entire campus impacted for Christ. Justin Christopher has done a wonderful job keeping the profound message in this book simple, yet insightful and engaging. May God raise up key people across the nation who will read and apply the truths in this book, so we can once again see Christ honored as King of kings and Lord of lords over the world of higher education."

DAVE WARN
Founder and Director, Collegiate Impact

Thanks

Special thanks to my wife, Brenda, who gives me peace each day by supporting me in my calling. She provides a loving home away from Campus Renewal Ministries and helps me take myself and the ministry less seriously.

Thanks to Campus Renewal Ministries staff, who have navigated this new ministry philosophy with me over these many years. Thanks to Jim Herrington, who helped us get started and whose continued blessing and encouragement have given me faith and courage to develop this movement at UT. Thanks to all the campus ministers and students (past, present, and future) at the University of Texas who are all a part of God's ongoing story at UT.

Special thanks to my ministry partners whose prayers and financial support are the backbone of everything that we are doing. This is your story too.

Thanks to my many friends who helped edit this book for content and clarity. Thanks to Deborah Costenbader for her copyediting and to Joel Skotak for his design work.

CONTENTS

FOREWORD

Every person who is interested in and committed to the transformation of culture in the United States should read Justin Christopher's book. We stand at an urgent crossroads and Justin has something to say to us all as we respond.

Twenty years ago there was an emerging awareness that we were losing the cities of our nation at supersonic speeds. Church membership and attendance were declining. The impact of the church in the public square took a sharp turn from a focus on character to a focus on politics. And societal trends like the divorce rate and the ubiquitous presence of poverty were gnawing away at the fabric of our society.

Twenty years later that emerging awareness has exploded into the failure of virtually every institution and system in our nation. Recently a leading pastor in Houston preached a sermon series entitled "Healing Broken America," announcing on billboards across the city what we all know in our hearts. Our culture is imploding around us and, if the trends of the past 20 years continue unabated for the next 20 years, we will have a mess indeed.

In the midst of this, Justin Christopher and a team of campus ministers at the University of Texas have been planting seeds and building a foundation that could contribute to the transformation of society in this next generation. There are at least three important things about what's happening at UT.

First, there is a prayerful, humble unity that has been patiently and painstakingly built over nearly 20 years. The psalmist says that in unity the blessing of God comes (Psalm 133). Though he would be the first to give credit to God and to the other campus ministers, Justin Christopher has been used by God to keep the flame of focused intercession alive on the campus for the past two decades. But this was not prayer for the sake of prayer. It was prayer that resulted in unity with a purpose. You'll enjoy reading how this has been worked out in a way that allows each ministry to maintain its unique identity while also developing a shared identity of the Church on the campus of UT. God is blessing this unity with increasing fruit.

Second, there is a thoughtful, strategic approach to the campus. These campus ministers have added mapping the campus to their praying. Through the *Longhorn Chronicles* they have mapped out their mission field so that they know who is on campus and where they are. This empowers the united team of campus ministries to prayerfully discern where God is at work and how they can join God there.

Third, there is a bold commitment to action. From its prayer and research, this group began planting missional communities on the campus. In a unified way, the campus ministers trained students to launch these communities in a growing number of dorms, clubs, groups, and component parts of the school. Today there are 220 missional communities embedded across the campus, and you'll be inspired by the stories of what God is doing through them.

I invite you to join me in imagining what could happen if one of the largest college campuses in the country was saturated with the salt and light of missional communities. What would the impact be as those missional community leaders graduate from UT and move to the cities of our nation in places of business, the arts, science, medicine, and academia? Now imagine that this is happening not just at UT, but at strategic campuses across the country. The impact would be enormous.

Justin has written a book that combines two things well. He reflects thoughtfully and accurately on the theology of reaching an entire campus. Then he artfully tells the unfolding story of how that theology has been turned into effective practice at UT. This book does not describe a new program that is replacing an old one. It describes the unfolding story of God's activity through these campus ministers and ministries on the UT campus over nearly 20 years. Justin tells the story with humility and conviction. I commend him and his book to you.

Jim Herrington
Mission Houston
July 2010

INTRODUCTION: In the Middle of It

A number of years ago I had the privilege of sharing a meal with Jackson Senyonga, a man featured in the Sentinel Group's *Transformations II* video that documents the amazing transformation taking place in Uganda. Jackson was one of the many pastors who spent years in prayer and partnership to see Kampala transformed by the gospel of Jesus. He had experienced revival firsthand. I asked him, "When did you know transformation had come to Uganda?" His answer confused me. He said, "After I watched the *Transformations II* video." I laughed and said, "How can that be? They came to shoot the documentary because they knew your country was being transformed." He replied, "I guess when you're in the middle of it, it does not seem as amazing, because you're still praying and seeking God for more. It was such a long process over so many years that we really had to stop and look back to see how far God had taken us." I found his comments profound and encouraging as I thought about my many years seeking God for transformation at the University of Texas. When would we know that revival had come? Maybe we were in the midst of it already.

I would certainly not claim that we are experiencing transformation at UT. If the folks from the Sentinel Group came to film a documentary of our work at UT, I'd suggest they wait until transformation has really come. That said, every time I tell the story of what God is doing at UT, people are amazed and want to know more: students and pastors are praying together every week, students are uniting to pray for revival 15 to 20 hours a day in a Campus House of Prayer, and several times a year many ministries cancel their normal activities to join together in worship and outreach. Formerly competitive ministries are now treating UT like one mission field by attempting to connect their students across ministry lines to be missionaries in fraternities, sororities, sports teams, clubs, ethnic student associations, dorms, cooperative living houses, and classrooms. People are excited about the obvious changes on our campus. In 2004, 5.5 percent of UT students were involved in our campus ministries, but now in 2010, 9.9 percent are involved in campus ministry. When I tell people that from 2001 to 2005 an average of 322 students a year put their faith in Jesus, but from 2006 to 2010 an average of 494 students become followers of Christ each year, people ask me how that is possible.

Over the last few years, after hearing more about our story, many people have responded, "You should write a book about that." Our story seems to be an encouragement to everyone who hears it, helping people think about a new way to approach reaching campuses with the gospel. Writing a book to tell our story seems like the best way to share what God has done at the University of Texas. My hope is that the students and ministers who read this book will grow in their faith to believe God will transform their campuses. I hope it will cause students and ministers to embrace a vision for the whole campus, not just their own campus ministry — that their vision would move from growing their ministries to literally reaching every student with the gospel of Jesus. I also hope this book will give ministry leaders practical strategies for reaching their campus together. These strategies have resulted in the increased impact we're having on campus.

"I GUESS WHEN YOU'RE IN THE MIDDLE OF IT, IT DOES NOT SEEM AS AMAZING, BECAUSE YOU'RE STILL PRAYING AND SEEKING GOD FOR MORE."

I am convinced that what took almost two decades to develop at UT can happen more quickly on other campuses. Years ago when we started this ministry, plans developed slowly through much prayer and conversation. We were attempting to do something that none of us had seen before, so we learned a lot along the way. Our story, I believe, will help other campuses move forward with a clearer vision from the start. As we continue to seek God together for transformation at the University of

Texas, we know that others are doing the same on their campuses. Some day we hope many campuses will have stories of transformation to tell — stories that bring glory to our Lord Jesus Christ.

Clarifying Some Terminology

Before you begin reading, I think it would be helpful to clarify a few terms that I use throughout the book. First, I will often use the pronouns "we" and "us." We and us do not refer to Campus Renewal Ministries staff or students. We and us refer to students and/or campus ministers from many different ministries. I am telling the story of how we, the whole Body of Christ, have been strategically working together to see the University of Texas transformed by the gospel of Jesus. We includes all of us.

I will also often use the terms "campus ministry" or "fellowship." By this I mean parachurch and church-based ministries that are reaching out to the University of Texas. Currently at UT, there are 63 church and parachurch groups. These include familiar parachurch groups like Campus Crusade for Christ and Navigators, denominational alliances such as the Baptist Student Ministry and the Wesley Foundation, several student-led Christian organizations, and several dozen local churches that have collegiate ministries (more than 35 churches in Austin have campus ministries at UT). I will refer to all of these organizations as campus ministries or fellowships. Similarly, I will refer to campus ministers and pastors interchangeably. By ministers and pastors I mean those men and women who lead a campus ministry (church or parachurch).

Campus Renewal Ministries

Finally, I would like to mention Campus Renewal Ministries (CRM), the ministry for which I work. Campus Renewal Ministries forges partnerships through prayer to build missional communities that transform college campuses with the gospel of Jesus Christ. My friend Jeremy Story and I founded CRM. We started the movement together as students at UT. After graduation, I stayed at UT to direct the movement locally, while Jeremy worked on a national level, helping start movements like ours on other campuses. As you will read, our ministry was blessed tremendously by consulting with Jim Herrington. It helped to have someone outside of our campus ministries to consult with us. We believe this will be true for your campuses as well, and we want to offer our services to you if you are inspired by the stories told in this book. Our staff is available to visit your campus to help the Body of Christ prayerfully consider how to partner together in prayer and mission. We also have many resources available online at www.campusrenewal.org. In addition, we have found that the type of united movement described in this book is enhanced significantly when there is someone on campus whose full-time job is providing leadership to the united effort. CRM would be happy to support anyone whom God has called to undertake this vision full-time. We already support staff on several campuses around the nation.

I pray that this story brings honor to God and encourages you. God is always at work. He has not left our campuses behind. Throughout history God has used students to bring awakening to their campuses, cities, and nations. He is not done yet.

VISION for **CAMPUS RENEWAL**

HOPE for OUR CAMPUSES

The University of Texas is thought by many to be the most liberal campus in Texas, which still feels like the "Bible Belt" compared to other parts of the United States. Often, well-meaning Christian parents have some fear about their kids coming to UT. Many encourage their children to go to more conservative schools like Baylor or Texas A&M. The typical comment heard by a high school graduate who tells someone in their youth group that he is going to UT is: "Oh, I will pray for you!" They mean well with their words, but in these words they speak unbelief. Jesus said, "out of the overflow of the heart the mouth speaks" (Matthew 12:34). Christian students, when they do come to UT, come with what I call a "retreat mentality." By that I mean they come to UT thinking, "I may lose my faith, so I had better find a Christian community to protect me." Yet scripture leaves no place for retreat. We are to have an "advancement mentality," because the gates of hell will not prevail against the church (Matthew 16:18). Gates are for defense. They are meant to stop invaders. The enemy is on the defense. We are advancing. This is Jesus's promise — that we will prevail against the enemy, bringing life and salvation to our campuses, even those perceived to be the farthest from God.

GOD IS PATIENT, CONTINUALLY WORKING TO REDEEM ALL PEOPLE GROUPS. WE KNOW THIS IS TRUE, IF ONLY BECAUSE THE END HAS NOT YET COME.

Students and campus pastors at UT have come to believe Jesus's promise. As a result, God is at work in tremendous ways.

God is always at work. He will continue to write His story until the time comes for the earth to burn away and the new heaven and new earth to be created. This is His promise. "The Lord is not slow in keeping his promise. He is patient with you, not wanting anyone to perish, but everyone to come to repentance" (II Peter 3:9). This is why He is waiting. God is not finished redeeming and transforming those whom He created. "This gospel of the kingdom will be preached in the whole world as a testimony to all nations, and then the end will come" (Matthew 24:14). God is patient, continually working to redeem all people groups. We know this is true, if only because the end has not yet come.

This has always given me reason for hope. It makes me see things differently. I realize that God's story is still being written, which means He is still working in my family and friends. There is reason for me to have hope for them and to continue to seek

God for their salvation and transformation. As a campus minister at the University of Texas, this also gives me hope for my campus. The promise is also true for this community of 50,000 students and 20,000 faculty, staff, and administration. God is patient with all 70,000 of them. His "tolerance and patience" is leading them to repentance (Romans 2:4). This makes it easy for me to wake up every day and trust that my life will cross the life of someone in whom God is already working. It makes it easy to mobilize students and ministers at UT toward a belief that God can once again bring renewal to our campus, as He has done so often in the past. God is patiently waiting for renewal at the University of Texas. So am I.

This is not to say that there are not reasons for being concerned or discouraged. When CRM is invited by other campus ministry leaders to visit their campuses, we ask them to give their best guess at the percentage of students involved in campus ministries. In almost every case they believe less than 5 percent of students on their campus are a part of their fellowships. The Barna Research Group studies indicate that 80 percent of high school graduates who attended church do not connect with churches in college.

These statistics should cause great alarm indeed, but even more, they should motivate us to "sound the alarm" (Joel 2:1). This should cause us to seek our patient God. "Even now, re- turn to me with all of your heart, with fasting and weeping and mourning. Rend your heart and not your garments. Return to the LORD your God, for he is gracious and compassionate, slow to anger and abounding in love, and relents from showing calam- ity. Who knows? He may return and have pity and leave behind a blessing" (Joel 2:12–14). Too often we wring our hands in fear over our condition, and we are tempted to lose hope, give up, or just maintain the status quo, happy to protect whatever small flock of students comes to us. Even though there is cause for con- cern, there is always hope. As Ezra's community said, "We have been unfaithful to our God by marrying foreign women from the peoples around this. But in spite of this, there is still hope for

Israel" (Ezra 10:2). While our universities are often scorned as places of idolatry and immorality, there is still hope for our campus for at least two reasons: who God is and what He is doing.

Hope Because of Who God Is

The foundation for hope for our campuses is the character of God. The root of hope can be founded in nothing less. Christian hope is not a worldly hope in the sense of crossing our fingers and wishing something would happen. Christian hope is a confident assurance in God, in His very person and in His word, which flows from who He is. Therefore, if we have any hope at all, it must be founded in the very nature of God and the promises that flow out of His person. There are at least three reasons to have hope for renewal on our campuses based on who we know God to be.

We Hope Because God Is Almighty

We hope because God is almighty, which means He's always able to transform us. God can do anything. Our campuses never reach a point that is beyond God's ability to transform. He is able to "give life to the dead and call things that are not as though they were" (Romans 4:17). God knew Abraham and Sarah's ages, but He could give life to the dead womb and call things that others said "were not" as though they "were indeed." We are the only ones who limit what God can do. He is able to do whatever He desires, and He is happy to wait for our faith to grow in order to do what He desires through us. God is fully able to change the whole spiritual climate of our campuses, no matter what the current statistics or reasons are that lead us to believe otherwise. Remember how the disciples were discouraged when Jesus spoke about how difficult it was for a rich man to enter heaven? They asked Jesus, "Who then can be saved?" Jesus answered, "With man this is impossible, but with God all things are possible" (Matthew 19:25–26). He is almighty, so He is always able to do miraculous work on our campuses.

When we first started our ministry at UT, one of the first things we had to do was to get students and ministers to believe again that God could transform the campus. Every Christian leader would verbally assent to God's power to change UT, but years of laboring and discouragement allowed doubt to creep into their hearts. We simply reengaged their hopes by looking at what God has done in His word and throughout history. We watched videos about the history of revival on college campuses in America, as well as the Sentinel Group's *Transformations* videos. Mostly, we united leaders each week in prayer, using scriptures of hope to direct our prayers. After a few years of prayer, students and ministers believed in their hearts, not just in their minds, that God has the power to transform our campus.

We Hope Because God Is Gracious

We hope because God is gracious, which means we're never beyond His reach. God's grace always triumphs over sin. Our campuses never reach a point where we can say, "We're too far gone," because "where sin increased, grace increased all the more" (Romans 5:20). God's grace is greater than the deceptive worldviews and the increased immorality on our campuses. God's grace is greater than the sins of any individual or any generation. His grace can redeem an individual and a generation, no matter what their sins and strongholds are. Paul said, "Here is a trustworthy saying that deserves full acceptance: Christ Jesus came into the world to save sinners — of whom I am the worst. But for this very reason I was shown mercy so that in me, the worst of sinners, Christ Jesus might display his unlimited patience as an example for those who would believe on him and receive eternal life" (I Timothy 1:15–16). Even Paul, a murderer of Christians, was not beyond God's grace. Nor are our campuses. If anything, as He did with Paul, God may choose the "worst" campus to display His glory. Our campuses are never beyond redemption, because God's grace is greater than all of our sin.

In 2010, the University of Texas was voted by *Playboy* magazine to be the number-one party school in the country. The article said, "When you add up academics, the weather, the liberal atmosphere, South by Southwest, game day and the nightlife on Sixth Street, UT Austin is one heck of a school." I compare that study with ours that shows during the same year 625 students put their faith in Jesus. Our statistics also show that there are more campus ministries at UT (63) than at any other campus I know, including 14 new ministries over the last four years. Very few campuses have as many students being saved or as many ministries focusing their efforts on students as we do at UT. God may be pleased, as He was in Paul's life, to transform the "worst of campuses" to glorify Himself and His grace.

We Hope Because God Is Patient

We hope because God is patient, which means He's willing to wait. God's patience is ultimately for one thing only — that we may repent and come to eternal life. As stated earlier, God would have created the new heaven and earth already if He were not waiting patiently and continuing His work. This should give us the utmost hope for our campuses. God is waiting, which means there is still hope. It is always in His heart to save and transform. His arms are always extended for students and our campuses. God is like the father of the prodigal who is patiently waiting with anticipation for his son's return (Luke 15). God is patient, and He continues to wait for our campuses to return to Him.

We have been working at this vision for almost 20 years. That's a long time! Surely God is patient with our campus and with us, the leaders of the Body of Christ at UT. We're still wrestling with what God is calling us to do together, but we do so with a firm belief that God is patient and that His kindness is leading us to repentance (Romans 2:4). It's His patience that allows us to persevere together. We are both working hard and waiting patiently for God to bring renewal to our campus.

Hope Because of What God Is Doing

Our hope is in God. He is the only One able to transform our campuses. We rest in His character above all things, but I believe that there is another reason to hope. I believe that there is evidence of God's grace, might, and patience already at work in tangible ways among this generation of students and campus ministers. I have been in campus ministry at the University of Texas since 1991 and have witnessed some specific reasons for hope, especially over the last few years. In addition, I have worked with several other leaders on a national level who also believe that God is up to something unique among this generation of students.

We Hope Because God Is Unifying This Generation

For a long time campus ministries competed with one another. Students would talk among themselves about why their ministry was better than others in its theology, methodology, and convictions. Church-based ministries tried to convince students that they needed to be part of a multigenerational church. Parachurch groups downplayed the role of churches, given that so few actually did anything to reach students on campus. Evangelicals prided themselves in their teaching and personal evangelism, charismatics in their praying and prophetic ministry, and denominational leaders in their service and compassion ministries.

The reason these well-meaning ministries found themselves in constant comparison with one another is that they were competing for the same students every year. As every campus minister knows, his or her ministry is just one freshman class away from extinction. Each fall, campus ministries compete for the loyalty of freshmen students who come to the university from Christian homes and youth groups. Add to this the fact that Christian students often move from one ministry to another over the course of their years at the university, based solely on which ministry has the best worship leader or best teacher, and the stage is set for the enemy to pit ministries against one another.

Something has changed in recent years, however, causing students and ministers to work with one another across ethnic, denominational, and theological lines. It's not that they have set out to work together; it's that these ministries have shifted their focus. Instead of trying to bring Christian freshmen into their ministries, now they are focused on connecting with students on campus who are far from God. Therefore, they are not competing to connect with the 500 new freshmen that come from Christian homes (they are doing that too, but with a different spirit). Instead, they are focusing their attention on reaching the 40,000 lost students on their campus. The shift in focus alone has drawn leaders together in a larger vision, one that compels them to be in relationship with one another.

This is not unity for unity's sake. It is unity based on a common mission and a humble recognition of a need for one another. A new generation of students and ministers are leading our campus ministries. They are more willing than ever to put aside denominational and organizational alliances for the sake of their mission to the campus. Students, especially, see themselves as followers of Jesus on their campus — not as Baptists, charismatics, Presbyterians, Methodists, Crusaders, or Navigators. They no longer draw those distinctions or have those exclusive allegiances. This is not to say that they are unaware of differences that they have in theology or practice, or even that they do not hold deep convictions. It's just that students in this generation do not let these differences keep them from meaningful relationships and partnerships in mission.

Things that used to divide, like styles of prayer or evangelism and ministry philosophies of specific organizations and denominations, no longer seem to matter to this generation. There is a new posture before one another, a willingness to listen and learn from each other. I see this particularly among students and younger campus ministers. Every week I participate in some prayer gathering or conversation that simply would not have happened years ago. I see students and ministers in settings that are very different from what they are accustomed to: a prayer meeting that gets a little loud, a conversation in which terms are used that once caused conflict or confusion, or a meeting about an issue that many ministries were not concerned about before. Yet the posture in the room is one of learning, appreciation for one another, and a conviction that we are the Body of Christ on our campus, called to work with one another to reach every lost community of students with the gospel.

Jeremy Story, the president of Campus Renewal Ministries, has traveled around the United States over the last 15 to 20 years. He can give testimony, better than anyone I know, of how this generation of students and ministers are coming together across ministry lines for the sake of their campuses. Below, he describes what God has been doing in campus ministry in recent years.

Stories of Campus Ministry Partnerships

We first started forging partnerships between various campus ministries and churches almost two decades ago. At that time leaders primarily wanted us to explain why localized and strategic campus-wide partnerships *should* be pursued; now leaders want us to show them how such partnerships *can* be pursued. The movement to prioritize partnership among leaders across our nation and the world is one of the most important paradigm shifts in modern campus ministry and in the church as a whole.

The past two decades provide numerous examples of how God has been reinstating a vision for intense partnership on individual campuses all across the country. During that time I have traveled to nearly every state in America and four other continents working with students and college ministry staff. I can tell you firsthand that in most every place the focus on partnership is growing.

Early on, many of these partnerships were more tactically oriented and usually focused around a particular campus-wide event. In the late '90s when Campus Renewal Ministries launched Resurrection Week, over 100 campuses and 30,000 students participated across the nation.

For many campus ministry leaders it was their first taste of working directly and intentionally with leaders from other

Christian churches and organizations on their campus. Students gathered outdoors and in major auditoriums on their campuses to pray and worship. They also spread out to serve the homeless and share the gospel with fellow students.

Around the same time the Veritas Forum movement began to take shape. My friend, Kelly Monroe, hosted the first Veritas Forum at Harvard and soon various campus ministries were joining together on campuses nationwide to influence the academic conversation itself. Since that time, it has been a regular occurrence on many campuses to host weeklong Veritas Forums to bring the brightest Christian thinkers to speak to large crowds of students and faculty.

Over time this vision for partnership has become more and more strategic rather than based on a single event. The goal has increasingly become partnering all year long to transform our nation's institutions of higher learning.

In the summer of 2005, students participating in our Ambassador network from across the nation gathered at Ohio State University. Most of them were leading ongoing united efforts on their campuses. God gave them the vision of working together nationally to launch a 24/7 prayer room which enabled continual prayer from campus to campus for an entire semester. Campus Church Network, 24-7 Prayer, and Burning Hearts Ministry all joined in the effort. We were amazed to see not only every day of the semester covered in prayer, but most of the time there were two to as many as eight or nine campuses hosting 24-hour-a-day prayer rooms on the same dates!

In addition to the University of Texas, campuses like the University of Tennessee, Ohio State University, Arizona State University, and Dartmouth have become shining examples of the power of year-round intentional partnerships. Leaders on these campuses, plus many others, have formed what Campus Renewal Ministries calls Fusion Groups. Groups of leaders meet regularly (often weekly) to pray and plan together to see more students reached with the gospel.

This passion for partnership has even reached to the national executive leadership of parachurch and denominational ministries. I currently meet with two different groups of national leaders annually to pray and share our lives together. These two meetings represent almost every national campus ministry leader in America. They are life giving, transparent meetings, not just lip service. Each of us shares deep personal ministry struggles and successes and prays for one another. All of us would say it is one of the more significant meetings we attend each year.

These are just a few of the hundreds of examples which reveal the national scope of God's move to call His people to partnership on college campuses. It is an encouraging trend which is spreading beyond college ministries and national boundaries.

We Hope Because God Is Calling Students to Pray

For a long time, prayer in our campus ministries was relegated to a weekly meeting that often consisted of 55 minutes of talking followed by 5 minutes of prayer. The prayer meeting was the smallest corporate gathering within each ministry and was usually led by one student who had the conviction to pray but was not fully supported by his or her campus minister. Rarely was prayer incorporated into the DNA of the ministry to the extent that prayer became a significant part of every gathering. Few ministries had times of extended prayer like a corporate fast or an entire night devoted to prayer. Now, however, these are commonplace.

Never before has there been as many students praying for their campuses as there are today. In February 2010, nearly 200 campuses participated in the Collegiate Day of Prayer, each having some sort of united prayer gathering on their campus. Thousands of students have been impacted by the ministry of the Campus Renewal Ministries, the International House of Prayer, Campus America, The Call, and Passion, each in their own unique way calling students to united prayer for awakening on their campuses. Many campuses now have campus houses of prayer where students from various ministries come to pray day and night. There are weekly united prayer times for students and campus ministers, when people from a variety of ministries come together to pray for awakening on their campuses. A number of ministries regularly promote seasons of prayer and fasting, making prayer a part of their corporate identity, even building prayer events into their calendars. Students are not praying out of guilt or obligation. Rather, there is a hunger for more of God and a faith in God to do something great on their campuses. Hunger is what compels them to pray.

This prayer movement is not unlike that of those who have gone before us and experienced campus awakening. As revival historian J. Edwin Orr famously said, "When God wants to bring revival, He always sets His people praying." This should give us great hope for our campuses. Students and ministers are uniting in prayer like never before.

STUDENTS ARE NOT PRAYING OUT OF GUILT OR OBLIGATION. RATHER, THERE IS A HUNGER FOR MORE OF GOD AND A FAITH IN GOD TO DO SOMETHING GREAT ON THEIR CAMPUSES.

Trent Sheppard is part of a collegiate prayer movement called Campus America. Campus America is an initiative of 24/7 Prayer International (UK) that helps students create dynamic prayer rooms on campus that last anywhere from 12 hours to 40 days. It's obvious to Trent, from what he has written below, that God is calling students to pray in an extraordinary way. The following stories of student prayer are taken from his book, *God on Campus: Sacred Causes & Global Effects*.

Stories of Student Prayer Across Campus America[1]

"We pray for the big things…we pray for the small things. It's just a bunch of people hungry for God."

Slate Stout, a student at Arizona State University, in *USA Today*[2]

Campus America — which is an abbreviated way of saying: every college and university campus in the United States — is at a moment of profound potential. Why? Because people are praying. People are engaging with God again. The soul of our universities is beginning to stir. Students and professors, young and old, the powerful and the poor: each in their own way are seeking for something more solid than the shaky commitment of the stock market, something more lasting than the wonderful but fragile ideals of democracy, something immeasurably more sacred than a "Christian" nation.

Arizona State University (ASU) is one of the biggest campuses in the country. More than fifty-one thousand students are enrolled at ASU. In the autumn of 2007, two hundred students at Arizona State determined to cover their campus in prayer for twenty-one days. "All through the day and night," reported an article in *USA Today* that covered the event, "they pray...their stillness and quiet in marked contrast to the nearly constant rush of...the campus."[3]

Three months after the event at ASU, *The Michigan Daily* covered a similar story at the University of Michigan (UM). Students at UM were involved in a project on campus called "40 Days of Prayer." The report in the *Daily* particularly highlighted the testimony of a sophomore, "who...passionately spoke to a captivated crowd about how the 40 Days of Prayer helped her overcome an eating disorder."[4] Multiple groups on campus, including Phi Alpha Kappa, Campus Crusade, World Reach International and New Life Church, sponsored the 2008 event. (One year later, when the event took place again, twenty campus groups were part of the prayer initiative.[5])

Just one month after the 40 Days of Prayer launched at UM in 2008, the *Columbus Dispatch* reported an incredible story that took place at Ohio University. "When an...employee decided to end his life Friday," the article explains, "students turned to the power of prayer and the pen to save him. It worked."[6]

According to the *Dispatch*, a group of praying students asked God to give them words of encouragement for a suicidal man who was preparing to jump from the ledge of a building on campus. A crisis specialist read the words of encouragement to the distraught man during a four-hour suicide intervention that ultimately saved his life. The following are excerpts from what the *Dispatch* called the "Samaritans' Letters":

I know sometimes it is easy to feel alone in the world, but it is important to remember that there are people who care. Right now there are a lot of people praying for you....You are not alone, and you are loved.

I don't know you or what is on your mind....But I do know the pain and brokenness that comes from living in this world. I have suffered from depression for two years, and I know what it feels like to be hopeless at times. But I know there is more. There is beauty. You'll see it if you look.

When people pray on campus, things begin to change. At the sprawling campus of Arizona State, this change looked like stillness in the midst of the mad hustle and bustle of fifty-one thousand students. At the University of Michigan it looked like a young woman set free from an eating disorder. At Ohio University it looked like a suicidal employee listening to the words of life when he was on the very edge of death. The power of prayer changes things.

At McDaniel College in Maryland this looked like thirteen students deciding to follow Jesus. At Haskell Indian Nations University in Kansas it looked like a young Caucasian woman and an older Native American intercessor weeping together over the sins of history. At Oklahoma State University it looked like a bunch of guys transforming a nineteen-bedroom frat house into a counter-culture of Christ-centered community and 24-7 prayer called The Jesus House. The power of prayer changes things.

At Morgan State University, a historically African American institution, this looked like a prayer tent in the center of campus with young black students on their knees in the middle of a late night storm. At Gardner-Webb University in North Carolina it looked like "a prayer room covered in art and scriptures, a wailing wall with...heart cries to the most holy God, a place where students could go spend time with their Creator."[7]

> *Those that visited the room encountered a wall of prayers and petitions. Real, raw prayers asking God for deliverance from sexual addictions, for suicidal thoughts, healing and release from illness, the salvation of lost friends. They found books full of prayers... They were able to see maps covered with pictures and writing and prayers for different parts of the world. Markers and colored pencils were scattered on the floor from where people had written verses on the wall. From where people had written, "Come, Lord Jesus, Come!"*[8]

Students are beginning to realize that the power of prayer changes things. They are also beginning to understand that the movement of prayer currently building across the campuses of America must be worked out in practical faith — a faith that makes sense to students and professors, parents and teachers, plumbers and scientists, architects and flight attendants — or else the movement will die as quickly as it comes.

"So here's what I want you to do," Paul said in Romans, "God helping you: Take your everyday, ordinary life — your sleeping, eating, going-to-work, and walking-around life – and place it before God as an offering" (Romans 12:1, *The Message*). The goal is not for us to abandon our studies in economics or education, for example, and become preachers instead. The goal is to live like Jesus in the very soul of society.

History alone will judge the faithfulness of our response to this calling. We will not be judged by how many people we pack into our prayer rooms or by how many converts we can record. Rather, history will judge our generation by whether or not the fruit we produce is the sort that lasts. Some dreams, like trees, are destined to die simply because they do not have roots that are deep enough to live. Other dreams, like Dr. Martin Luther King's, may take a long time to grow into fullness, but their lasting effect is historic.

That is the sort of dreaming required for our day. Generous dreams that freely merge the great divide between the powerful and the poor. Broken dreams that understand what it practically means to sacrificially give our lives away in the service of others. Holy dreams that are not bound by sacred rooms or limited to mystical experiences, but the sort of dreams that are set free to reimagine what a redeemed humanity might truly be in everyday, extraordinary life.

We Hope Because God Is Calling Students to Mission

For a long time campus ministries mostly functioned as safe places for Christian students at their universities, leading to the competition for incoming students. Emphasis was placed on meeting freshmen early in the fall and then expending time, money, and energy creating a vibrant weekly meeting. Students who came to the large group meeting were strongly encouraged to join small groups where they could be discipled and hopefully become small group leaders the next year. Evangelism, then, was mostly about trying to get students to bring their friends to the large group meeting. To be fair, some ministries were active in "contact evangelism" on campuses, but (like the prayer meeting) this usually involved only a few students who cared about evangelism going out in pairs once a week to share their faith with others. Evangelism became the work of a small team of students and others willing to invite friends to a really well-done weekly meeting. The problem, however, was that fewer and fewer unchurched students each year were interested in attending a worship service and even fewer Christian students were interested in doing contact evangelism.

More recently campus ministers are recognizing that to reach students who are far from God, they need to equip their students to go to the lost communities, rather than asking their friends to come to them. Students, at the same time, are looking for a more authentic way to engage their friends, and they want to have friendships outside of their Christian communities. These changes are paving the way for a new type of evangelism on campus — something that involves every Christian student, not a select few. A way that asks them to go to the lost, instead of asking the lost to come to them.

THESE CHANGES ARE PAVING THE WAY FOR A NEW TYPE OF EVANGELISM ON CAMPUS — SOMETHING THAT INVOLVES EVERY CHRISTIAN STUDENT, NOT A SELECT FEW. A WAY THAT ASKS THEM TO GO TO THE LOST, INSTEAD OF ASKING THE LOST TO COME TO THEM.

Ministries like Campus Renewal Ministries and Campus Church Network are teaching students to be missionaries on campus to specific people groups. Larger campus ministries like Campus Crusade for Christ and InterVarsity Christian Fellowship offer ethnic-specific ministries to reach certain people groups. They are changing the aim of their efforts to start "multiple movements" on campuses rather than one large movement with one weekly large group meeting. The "score card" for campus ministry success is changing from one that measures how many students are coming to our events to one that measures how many different areas of the campus are students impacting with the gospel. For many years, the cultural and relational gap between believing and unbelieving students was growing; now it is narrowing, creating opportunities for the gospel to touch many more students' lives.

Jaeson Ma, founder of Campus Church Networks, has traveled to college campuses around the world to encourage students to live on mission. His exhortation to students at UT in 2007 resulted in the birth of 60 new missional communities to specific parts of our campus. He believes that God is cultivating a new generation of believers ready to go to the lost, instead of staying isolated within their Christian bubbles. In his book *The Blueprint: A Revolutionary Plan to Plant Missional Communities on Campus,*[9] he writes the following:

Stories of Students on Mission

On college and university campuses all across North America and other nations there has been a sweeping move of 24/7 campus houses of prayer. We have recorded reports of non-Christian students experiencing the presence of God through power evangelism encounters on numerous campuses. At the same time, a new generation of leaders is being commissioned in the power of the Holy Spirit from the campus into every sphere of society. More and more, Christian students are realizing that they are not on campuses just to fellowship but also to be campus missionaries. They are invading lost pockets of unreached student groups on campus and planting simple churches or missional communities among the lost. We must have a passion to see these strategies mobilized, but we must first understand the reality of what the Church is up against in this generation. This is the blueprint. This is God's game plan to release an apostolic and prophetic generation to fulfill the Great Commandment and finish the Great Commission.

If we want to see God's power show up in this generation, it will take drastic change. It will take our first changing our hearts. It will require our humbling ourselves before Almighty God, turning from our wicked ways and releasing a desperate cry for revival (see II Chronicles 7:14). It will require praying as if all depends on God and living as if it all depends on us. Prayer brings revival. Action brings reformation. We need both desperately.

God is calling forth a generation that is passionate for His presence. A generation that knows who they are and Whose they are. He is calling forth sons and daughters who don't find their identity in revival but in Christ. For the Great Commission must flow out of the Great Commandment. Our destinies must flow out of our identities as beloved children of God who know their worth, value and honor before their Father. Out of this place of rest will flow the greatest revival in human history. We are sons and daughters first, revivalists second. We have nothing to prove and nothing to lose. God is raising up a student-led army that is passionate for prayer, power evangelism and planting simple churches in this end-time hour. It is time for change. It is time for revival and reformation in this generation.

The Power of a Student Movement

Campus ministry is tiring work. There is little glory for campus pastors. Many have to raise their own money in order to do the ministry. Then there is the annoying fact that 25 percent of the ministry leaves every year (students graduate). It's like you hit the reset button every fall and move through seasons of momentum and decline each semester until it is time to hit the reset button again. Why do we do it? Because we are convinced that students can change the world. It has been true throughout history. Students do change history. It is true for God's purposes, such as the Student Volunteer Movement in the late 1800s that raised up thousands of missionaries from our country. It is also true for the enemy's purposes, as seen in the sexual revolution in the '60s and '70s. As our campuses go, so goes the world.

Almost all of our future leaders in government, education, business, and entertainment come from our universities (nationally and internationally). If the Church loses its impact on our universities, it loses its impact on the world. That's why campus ministers from Campus Crusade for Christ, InterVarsity Christian Fellowship, Navigators, Every Nation Campus Ministry, International Students Incorporated, Chi Alpha, Wesley Foundation, Baptist Student Ministry, and many local denominations and fellowships in college towns have given themselves fully to the discipleship of college students. They are convinced that if we can reach the campus, we can reach far beyond it. So many ministers have worked tirelessly for years and decades to see their campuses changed in the hope that their students would then reach the world.

I am proud to have worked side by side with many of these committed leaders for nearly 20 years now. We are hopeful that God will do something historic at the University of Texas, for His glory. We've yet to see our hope realized, but we believe we are on our way, and we are deeply committed to seeking God together for His plan to reach campuses in our generation. God is still able to transform our campuses. He is already moving in significant ways. There is reason to hope and pray for more.

---

1. "Stories of Student Prayer Across Campus America" is adapted from *God on Campus: Sacred Causes & Global Effects*, by Trent Sheppard. Copyright © 2009 by Trent Sheppard. Used by permission of InterVarsity Press, PO Box 1400, Downers Grove, IL 60515. www.ivpress.com.

2. John Faherty, "Ariz. Students Organize Prayer Marathon," *USA Today* (Nov. 2, 2007), accessed May 27, 2009, at <www.usatoday.com/news/religion/2007-11-02-prayermarathon_N.htm?POE=click-refer>.

3. Ibid.

4. Jillian Berman, "Student groups kick off 40 days of prayer: Christian groups unite in effort to show power of communal prayer," *The Michigan Daily* (Jan. 14, 2008), accessed May 27, 2009, at <www.michigandaily.com/content/student-groups-kick-40-days-prayer>.

5. Veronica Menaldi, "Campus Christian groups unite for 40 day prayer marathon," *The Michigan Daily* (Jan. 8, 2009), accessed May 27, 2009, at <www.michigandaily.com/content/2009-01-09/ campus-christian-groups-unite-40-day-prayer-marathon>.

6. Sherri Williams, "Answered prayers: Suicidal man persuaded to live," *The Columbus Dispatch* (Feb. 10, 2008), accessed May 27, 2009, at <www.dispatch.com/live/content/local_news/ stories/2008/02/10/samaritans_ou.html?sid=101>.

7. Tyler J. McCall, "Reigniting Prayer: A Report from Gardner-Webb University," on 24-7 Prayer's U.S. website (March 10, 2008), accessed May 28, 2009, at <www.24-7prayer.us/index. php?option=com_content&task=view&id=135&Itemid=114>. Articles about each of the campuses mentioned in this and the preceding paragraph are available in the "News" section of the website (www.24-7prayer.us).

8. Ibid.

9. Jaeson Ma, *The Blueprint: A Revolutionary Plan to Plant Missional Communities on Campus* (Ventura, CA: Regal Books, 2007).

the
UNIVERSITY of
TEXAS STORY

God is always at work. He was working
at the University of Texas before it
was even founded. After all, He is all-
knowing. He knew us before we were
born (Psalm 139), so He has known and
loved every student who has set foot
on our campus. I like to remind myself
of this fact, because my story, which
starts in 1991, is only a small fraction of
His work at UT. I have heard from many
others who have gone before me about

the great things God did while they were students. In fact, the local church that I am a part of started as a Bible study for students when I was just three years old! That's just going back 34 years, not the full 127 years since UT was first established. That's why I like to be careful not to portray this new movement as the only thing God has ever done on our campus. It's not. It's really just my perspective — a small window in time, a window of about 20 years. Before I tell about my many years of ministry at UT, however, I need to share how God prepared me for my time on campus, which takes me back to my freshman year in high school.

God Saves Me (1988)

I was a lonely teenager seeking to find my significance in football and friendships with the wrong people when I met Barry Bowling. He led the chapel service before one of my freshman football games. Barry was on staff with Student Venture (Campus Crusade's high school ministry), and he met with me the next week and invited me to a Bible study. Several of the football players I was trying to hang out with joined the study, so I thought I would too. After a few months of investigating what the Bible said about life, faith, and Jesus, I decided to attend the Student Venture summer camp. There at the YMCA of the Rockies I gave my life to the Lord and have been following Him ever since. Barry discipled me, showing me how to develop my relationship with God and teaching me how to share the gospel with my teammates on the football team (my mission field).

My Calling (1989)

A year later I attended another Student Venture conference that was focused on prayer and revival. Several speakers told about amazing things God was doing on high school and college campuses. A guy named Dan Hayes taught on principles for revival as seen in the Bible and through history. Much of what he said is contained in his book *Fireseeds of Spiritual Awakening*. I left that

conference in 1989 with a completely new vision for life, to live for Jesus and call others to revival on my campus. We started a weekly united prayer time called "pancakes and prayer" (trust me when I say we prayed a lot too). In addition, several of us started praying many mornings a week, even going out on campus to share our faith with classmates. Several players on my football team put their faith in Jesus, and I began leading them in Bible studies at my home. We all were a part of different churches, but we prayed together regularly and lived and shared the gospel with those in our spheres of influence. I am blessed to say that, thanks to Student Venture, this was the normal Christian life for me. It prepared me for what God had for me at UT.

Daily Prayer (1991)

I came to UT expecting God to move through me, and I was committed to finding others who expected the same. I lived with a few Student Venture friends my freshman year, and on Labor Day, we all decided to go to a conference to hear Dan Hayes. His stories of revival from scripture and history stirred up our faith and led us to want God to be glorified in the same way at UT. Every revival story that he shared began with a small group of students praying, so we figured we'd follow suit. We started praying daily at 7 A.M. (no one has class then!).

As usual, God was already working. The second week of our praying together several others called us up and said, "We've been praying for revival every day at 7 A.M. too. Can we pray together?" We praised God and said, "Of course!" We wanted our prayer time to include students from other ministries, and now it did. We were never a very large prayer group, but we were faithful. Though some the students changed from year to year, as they do in college ministry, a group of us met every day for all four years of my time as a student at UT, and even eight years beyond that, but we'll get to that later.

Our focus was simple. We met daily to share reports on what God was doing on campus and in the lives of the friends that we were praying for, to read scripture that could direct our prayers and build our hope for revival, and to pray those scriptures for our campus. It was just an hour a day, but it was and is the basis for all God is doing today at UT.

United Prayer (1992)

Our desire was to see believers from more ministries praying together. Our daily prayer group had students from about six different fellowships participating, but UT had around 30 different campus fellowships at the time. We felt led to contact students from these other campus ministries to invite them to a weekly united prayer gathering on Friday afternoons. The goal was to have at least one student from each ministry involved. We did not find a student from every ministry, but before the end of my sophomore year we had about 20 of the 30 ministries represented in this united prayer group. We directed the prayer much like we did each morning: sharing what God was doing on campus, reading a scripture or two, and then praying through the scriptures. We always made sure to pray for awakening, because we wanted at least one student from each ministry to grow in their faith and hunger for revival at UT. It did not take long for their faith and hunger to grow.

Concerts of Prayer (1993)

One week after the closing prayer of our united prayer meeting, a student said he thought God might be leading us to bring all of our ministries together for a night of united prayer. Everyone agreed that this was something God was calling us to do. Spring semester of my sophomore year several hundred people turned out for our first concert of prayer. There was no teaching that night, just an ebb and flow of prayer and worship (or what I like to call spoken prayer and singing prayer). It was all prayer — prayer directed at stirring hope in students for revival. We were trying to encourage a larger number of students on campus to

embrace the advancement mentality, to see themselves as missionaries to the campus, and to believe that God could use them to radically transform UT. We led concerts of prayer once or twice a semester for the next several years, and a much larger prayer movement was birthed. Thirty to 40 students joined us for daily prayer for weeks at a time. Students were joining us in the morning and leading their ministries' weekly prayer time on campus too. Many of the students who came to united prayer were also changing the hopes and prayers of students within their ministries. The student movement continued to grow, hitting a climax during my senior year. That led me to an important decision.

WE ALWAYS MADE SURE TO PRAY FOR AWAKENING, BECAUSE WE WANTED AT LEAST ONE STUDENT FROM EACH MINISTRY TO GROW IN THEIR FAITH AND HUNGER FOR REVIVAL AT UT.

Rez Week (1995)

My senior year I was contacted by a student named Jeremy Story. He had also been calling students from various ministries to pray together and to become involved in something called Rez Week (short for Resurrection Week): a week of united prayer, worship, fellowship, and outreach that takes place near Easter. We had the same heart and vision but had simply never met. Ironically, some of the ministries not represented in our weekly united prayer gathering were already a part of his, and vice versa. So we brought our groups together in prayer each week and began to work on the first Rez Week at UT. It was a fantastic week. Large numbers of students were touched by the gospel, and many put their faith in Jesus that week. Equally significant was what the event produced in the Body of Christ. There was an increased desire among students to continue to work as one Body to see the University of Texas transformed by the gospel. So much so, that I wondered, "Could this be a calling for me?"

After Rez Week, several pastors and ministry leaders in Austin heard about what we were doing. They told Jeremy and me that they would like to help support us, so that we could continue to lead the movement at UT. I jumped at the chance and immediately began raising funds. Jeremy, still a student, led the movement while I was away building my partnership team. Then, after Jeremy graduated, he too began raising support to continue this work full time. Some of the same ministry leaders in Austin helped Jeremy start his own 501(c)(3) organization, Campus Renewal Ministries, the one in which we and several others around the nation now serve. I stayed at UT to work, while Jeremy led the national movement first from Austin and then from where he now lives, in New York City.

Campus Minister Prayer (1997)

When I came back to Austin after a year of developing my partnership team, I knew the next step was to start a united prayer gathering for campus ministers, just like the one we had for students. This was much more difficult than getting the student group started. Campus pastors were more difficult to contact and meet in person, and some were a bit resistant to what we were doing (or as we later found out, what they perceived we were doing). The year that I was away raising my partnership team (1995–1996), Jeremy worked hard just to get the pastors to pray with one another once a month. After I returned, Jeremy and I spent the next year meeting with every pastor one on one to encourage them to begin praying together weekly, but it never took off. Finally, the following fall semester, a few key leaders thought it worthwhile to pull campus pastors together to at least talk about praying together. It was a historic meeting.

As we discussed things quite openly, three specific questions boiled to the top of the discussion: *Is this unity for unity's sake? Is it all going to be about events? Are we all going to look the same?* Over the years, ministers had seen students get really excited about unity. "Unity for what?" they always asked. In our mind, the goal was never unity. The goal was to see the transformation of the campus and to some day literally reach every unbelieving community on campus with the gospel. The goal was to see the campus transformed, not to unify. However, we needed to work together to see the campus transformed. This was not a matter of semantics. We did not want to unite for the sake of unity. We wanted to unite in order to reach the whole campus with the gospel. Clarifying this misunderstanding about unity brought a new perspective.

Through the years, ministers had worked together on various events. It usually came about when someone had an idea for an outreach that their ministry could not afford to do alone. So they would propose the idea to other pastors and form a committee to work on the event together. Their reason for meeting was the event. What we were proposing was much different. We were sure God would lead us at times to plan events, but the purpose of our meeting would be for prayer, not planning events. Our purpose for gathering was to get to know one another and to pray for awakening at UT. This was another important clarification.

WE DID NOT WANT TO UNITE FOR THE SAKE OF UNITY. WE WANTED TO UNITE IN ORDER TO REACH THE WHOLE CAMPUS WITH THE GOSPEL.

Finally, there was a little fear in the room concerning how we could pray and work together without watering down what made each ministry unique. We talked about this concern and simply agreed that we could best reach the campus if we maintained our differences and were who God called each of us to be. It was possible to pursue unity and maintain diversity in a way that honored each other and honored God. Ironically, after 13 years of praying together each week, something unexpected has occurred. Now that we know each other so well, we are more different than ever, but in a healthy way, with each ministry knowing its part in the Body of Christ.

After this initial conversation, we decided to begin praying together every week for a year. We said that we would convene again in the following May to determine if we would continue praying together. The funny thing was, we never met in May. After a year of praying together, it was obvious to everyone that we needed to continue. After a few years of praying together, our relationships and vision grew to a point where we were able to take a bold next step.

Campus Minister Council (2000)

After a few years of weekly prayer, there seemed to be a general sense that we needed to do more than pray and hold an occasional event together, but we were not sure what that meant. We called a meeting to talk about where God might be leading us. I had been reading a great book called *City Reaching* at the time and shared a little illustration from the book that described how to go from "tactical unity" to "strategic unity." The illustration seemed to speak directly to us because we wanted to find a more long-term, strategic way of mobilizing our ministries to reach the campus together. We all agreed to read the book and discuss it weekly. We jokingly call it the first UT miracle! Over the next three weeks we read the book, meeting once a week to discuss portions of it. Afterward, we felt like we had been given a road map for our desire to move beyond just prayer and events.

One of the contributing authors to *City Reaching,* Jim Herrington, lives in Houston. We asked him to come and consult with us, to spend a day helping us think through what city reaching might look like on campus. Praying together was one step, reading a book another, but 15 ministers spending half a day together to talk about long-term, strategic ways of mobilizing our students and resources to reach the campus together, now that was amazing! The first meeting with Jim set us on a course of writing a vision statement together: "Strategically working together to see the University of Texas community transformed by the gospel of Jesus Christ." Just the process of working through

a united vision statement was incredible. It set us on a unique course. We continued to invite Jim to meet with us for one or two days every October. Each year when we met with Jim at the Campus Minister Council, God would clearly direct us to a next step to take together.

Prayer Mobilization (2001)

In 2001, we came away from our time with Jim with a commitment to mobilize even more prayer on campus. That did not mean that we were making prayer a focus for one year, but that we were making a commitment over the long haul to build a growing, united prayer movement. By committing to prayer mobilization, we were determining that every time we met for a Campus Minister Council, we would ask, "What can we do this next year or two to continue to build into the united prayer movement at UT?" Over the years, God has led us to several initiatives to grow the prayer movement on campus.

The first has been to continue to pray together weekly, to have the students united in prayer each week also, and to have concerts of prayer once a semester. Some specific initiatives have included: "Adopt-a-Prof" prayer cards that coordinate prayer for all 3,000 professors at UT, "High-Five" cards that lead students to pray daily for five unbelieving friends that they see almost every day, and a week of 24-hour prayer in a tent in the middle of campus during Rez Week.

Our focus on building a growing movement of prayer led us in 2006 to start the Campus House of Prayer (CHOP), where students from all of our ministries unite in prayer for about 100 hours a week, and often for periods of 24/7 prayer. Students sign up online for an hour of prayer in the CHOP, and then keep that time for the entire semester. Most of our CHOP times are filled with students praying for their missional communities — their lost friends and the community of unbelievers of which they are a part.

Spiritual Mapping (2002)

The following year we left our time with Jim with a commitment to spiritually map our campus. Simply stated, that means we wanted to focus our effort on better understanding what God was doing on campus and what the enemy was doing on campus. We wanted to study the history of the University of Texas, create a year-end survey for every ministry to complete, survey our students to discover more about their spiritual condition, and understand more about the hundreds of people groups that existed at UT.

The simplest form of spiritual mapping had already been taking place as we brought leaders together to pray, share what God was doing, and talk about the spiritual state of UT. Conversations alone gave us a much clearer picture of what God was doing on campus. From this point on, however, we committed to do spiritual mapping in a more systematic way. The first thing we did was create a year-end survey that every ministry would complete, so that we could get a better statistical look at the Body of Christ at UT. We met several times to brainstorm what we wanted to know and to write specific questions. The first year-end survey was administered at the end of the 2002 spring semester. We collected the data, compiled it in a publication called the *Longhorn Chronicles*, and met the following October to read and discuss what we learned. Ever since, we have had a yearly gathering called the Campus Minister Luncheon where we discuss the latest edition of the *Longhorn Chronicles* and hear testimonies from dozens of campus ministries.

WE'RE CREATING A SPIRITUAL MAP SO THAT WE CAN REALLY KNOW WHAT GOD IS DOING ON CAMPUS, AND WHAT THE ENEMY IS DOING ON CAMPUS. OUR MAP DIRECTS OUR PRAYERS WHEN WE MEET EACH WEEK AND GUIDES OUR CONVERSATION WHEN WE COME TOGETHER TO PLAN.

In 2003, we added to our spiritual map by putting together a survey for the Christian students in our ministries. Again, we wrote it together, deciding what we wanted to ask and meeting again to formulate the questions. We administered the survey within individual ministries, so they could have a picture of their students and we combined all the surveys so that we could have a picture of the Body of Christ. The survey helped us understand where our students lived, what people groups they belonged to, what their family backgrounds were, where they struggled with addictions, how they used their time, and what their devotional lives were like. I will share more about the results in later chapters, but here I will tell you that we have made changes to our ministries based on what we have learned from these surveys. We continue to tweak this survey and administer it every four years, so that we can know more about each generation of students.

In 2004, we mobilized about 80 students from our ministries to conduct surveys on campus to get a better feel for the thoughts and feelings of those outside the Christian community. These 80 students conducted 10 interviews each at 80 different places on campus. The locations for the interviews were specifically chosen so that we could interview almost every UT demographic (every ethnicity, every dorm, every department, etc.). We did all of the interviews in one week, then debriefed together to share what we had learned. It was an eye-opening experience for the students who participated. We worked with an organization that compiled the data into a useable format for all ministries to use so that they could consider the people they were trying to reach and develop better plans to connect with them based on their specific needs. We've yet to do this again, but at our last Campus Minister Council meeting we decided to do something very similar in January of 2011.

Our spiritual map is continually being adjusted through conversations, research, and specific initiatives. We're creating a spiritual map so that we can really know what God is doing on campus, and what the enemy is doing on campus. Our map directs our prayers when we meet each week and guides our conversation when we come together to plan.

Missional Communities (2003)

The last extended time we spent with Jim Herrington resulted in our writing a powerful vision statement which read: "We want to see a viable Christian community in every college, club, residence, and culture at UT." We knew that we had to mobilize prayer, since we could do nothing without God. We wanted to develop our spiritual map of UT, so that we could operate as one Body with a clear understanding of what God and the enemy were doing at UT. Finally, we wanted to mobilize and network our students as missionaries to every people group on campus.

One thing made clear by our early spiritual mapping efforts was that we were not reaching unbelieving communities. Our surveys helped us conclude that we were not reaching lost communities at UT primarily because our students were involved in too many Christian activities and, as a result, were detached from unbelieving communities. This would never be tolerated on the mission field overseas. We thought we should not tolerate it on our campus either. So we began to call all of our students to connect with only one ministry, to find real community and discipleship there, but to also find one community of unbelievers and spend time within that community on mission with a few other believers. It is amazing what can happen when ministers unite to teach one message!

WE DON'T CARE ABOUT WHO "OWNS" THE MISSIONAL COMMUNITIES OR WHO GETS THE CREDIT FOR THEIR SUCCESS. WE CARE ABOUT SEEING EVERY PEOPLE GROUP REACHED AT UT.

In 2004, we commissioned our first official missional communities. About 20 teams were embedded within dorms, co-ops, sports teams, Greek houses, and specific colleges. The next year there were 40, the next 80, then 150, and now there are more than

220 active missional communities on the UT campus. We believe we need more than 500 to really reach the whole campus. That is our aim.

From 2004 to 2007 many ministries united to train their missional community leaders in one setting. Initially, we used material entitled "Retrospect," developed by a church planting trainer in Houston named Glenn Smith. No one knew how to equip their students for this new mission, so we partnered together until enough momentum and material were developed for each ministry to train their own students. A significant change occurred from 2007 to 2010, with more and more ministries equipping students to be missionaries to specific parts of campus. The leadership structure of many ministries has completely changed to make this a first priority — to go to the lost.

Most recently an incredible partnership has formed among 10 campus ministries (we're hopeful that more will join each year). The partnership is called Renovate UT. These 10 ministries have made a deeper commitment to the missional community movement. They meet for several hours once a month to share stories and communicate about who is doing what where and how we can connect our students. We even share a database with contact information of more than 140 missional communities at UT. We don't care about who "owns" the missional communities or who gets the credit for their success. We care about seeing every people group reached at UT.

Given that unbelieving communities often have students from many of our ministries in them, it makes the most sense to connect our students with each other if they share the same community of unbelievers. Several ministries have students in the nursing school, for instance. Renovate UT connects these students and makes sure that one ministry is providing some coaching. This summer we're having a united Renovate UT retreat, where campus ministers from these 10 ministries will team-teach and equip next year's missional community leaders. This is an amazing degree of partnership!

What God Has Accomplished

I will be the first to say that we're not there yet. We've yet to experience the revival we've been praying about for these many years. We also have not been able to reach every people group at UT with the gospel. All I can say is that we are on our way.

Leaders in the Body of Christ at UT pray together weekly and have humble, life-giving relationships with one another. We share a common vision to mobilize students in united prayer and mission so that we reach every unbelieving community on campus with the gospel and experience a historic revival. We have a more complete picture of what God is doing on campus and what role each of our individual ministries plays in the whole vision for transformation. Campus ministry leaders meet twice a semester for several hours to communicate and recalibrate our efforts. We are, indeed, working as one Body of Christ.

We feel like God has taken us to a new place, giving us a whole new way of doing ministry at the University of Texas. We believe we're in step with the Holy Spirit, and it is only a matter of time until we see the breakthrough. More important, we feel we're being faithful to our God as we humble ourselves before one another, working as one Body to reach the whole campus.

We're seeing God do the intangible things in us that He clearly requires before He brings revival, namely humility, hunger, prayer, and repentance. Jackson Senyonga once told us, "Humility is God's revelation of your need for one another." If that is God's definition, then we have grown to be quite a humble movement here at UT. New ministers come to UT and are amazed at the way we love and respect one another and continue to work together because we're convinced that we need each other.

As for hunger, it's obvious that God has given us a holy discontentment with things as they are. No one is satisfied with the thought of just shepherding the flock of students that comes to us. No one is trying to get the best worship leader or teacher so their ministry is the largest, taking students away from the other ministries. Instead, we want revival. We have a desire for God to do something at UT for which no one can take credit.

It's amazing that we have the Campus House of Prayer now. Prayer is not for the gifted or extra-spiritual students UT. Everyone is praying all over campus and 100 or more hours a week in the Campus House of Prayer. Students and campus ministers unite in prayer once a week and bring their ministries together in united prayer at least once a semester. We're praying like never before, and prayer always precedes revival.

As for repentance, we're on our way. Our spiritual map reveals to us ways we need to lead the Body of Christ in repentance. We base events around needs for repentance, and our prayers are often filled with identificational repentance. Ministry leaders are even in accountability relationships with one another so that we can hold each other accountable as leaders of this movement.

Our surveys indicate that God is already moving in significant ways. Here is a simple look at the three statistics we believe are most important. In 2002, 5.5 percent of UT students were involved in our campus ministries. In 2010, more than 9.9 percent are involved in our campus ministries. The Body of Christ at UT has almost doubled! From 2001 to 2005 we saw an average of 322 students put their faith in Jesus each year. From 2006 to 2010 an average of 494 students put their faith in Jesus each year. We're not just growing by transfer growth or incoming freshmen growth. The number of missional communities in 2003 was 20.

WE SHARE A COMMON VISION TO MOBILIZE STUDENTS IN UNITED PRAYER AND MISSION SO THAT WE REACH EVERY UNBELIEVING COMMUNITY ON CAMPUS WITH THE GOSPEL AND EXPERIENCE A HISTORIC REVIVAL. WE HAVE A MORE COMPLETE PICTURE OF WHAT GOD IS DOING ON CAMPUS AND WHAT ROLE EACH OF OUR INDIVIDUAL MINISTRIES PLAYS IN THE WHOLE VISION FOR TRANSFORMATION.

Now, in 2010, there are more than 220 missional communities. That means UT (which has an estimated 500 people groups) is nearly 50 percent reached, having a Christian community imbedded within half of the campus!

Perhaps it's not something Dan Hayes or J. Edwin Orr would write about just yet. It is, however, something rarely seen in campus ministry. It is, in our opinion, a new way forward. It is a new way of doing campus ministry. Many campus pastors already recognize the need for a new way forward. They just don't know how to get there. We hope that our story can pave a way, much like the ministry philosophy set forth in *City Reaching* paved the way for us.

" It's been said that 2 percent of an organization, if completely sold out to a particular vision, can change the entire organization. While I am not sure of the veracity of that fact, I can say from experience that just a few college pastors working together on a project (e.g., a mission trip or a campus event), attending a retreat, or uniting in prayer can have a marked effect on the direction of your entire campus movement.

At the University of Texas we can point to several such examples that were significant in the history of God's work on our campus. Some years ago we watched a couple of the *Transformations* videos and suddenly, those of us who watched them were challenged with the notion that God could do far more on our campus than we had dared to think or imagine. This emboldened us to pray toward a level of campus-wide transformation which we had not previously been able to conceive.

Later, a small group of eight pastors and three or four staff from CRM attended The Institute for Campus Revival and Awakening held at Yale. It resulted in a deepening of relationships with pastors from other groups that we had previously only known through prayer and common events. By the time the weeklong trip was over we had grown much closer as friends and had a new level of intimacy, which also increased our ability to pray for the campus and pray for each other.

These stories are only a couple of examples that represent quite a few more instances in which we found ways to work together outside of the weekly times of prayer. But the result has been a steady and increasing buy-in to what God is doing on our campus. Whereas before many of us could have been rightly described as skeptical of what God could do on our very secular campus, we have now seen God work in ways that increase our faith for what He is going to do in the future.

Since I have been on campus, we have seen our weekly pastor prayer time go from about four to eight pastors attending to about 20 to 30 pastors, and sometimes more! We have also just completed our fourth year of hosting the Campus House of Prayer where over 100 hours of prayer per week are typically covered. We have seen some of our dreams wildly surpassed and now we are dreaming new dreams!

Please don't underestimate how God can use your willingness to work with fellow leaders (whether students or staff) on your campus. And by all means, "don't despise the day of small beginnings" (Zechariah 4:10) because, just as God delights in growing a large tree from a small seed, He can do huge things through your working together as the Body of Christ on your campus. 🙶

MARK PROEGER
Hope Student Life
CAMPUS MINISTER, 2003–2010

the
CAMPUS-REACHING
MODEL

As I said earlier, I had a vision for this kind of ministry since I was in high school. Ever since I heard Dan Hayes speak about campus revivals, I have wanted to learn more from history. What did the stories have in common? What could we do to prepare for revival? What characterized the revival leaders' relationships with God? I have read numerous books about revival over the years; some that relayed the stories of revivals (past and present), some that gave principles and practices for revival, and many that did both. Of course, there is always a tension in reading about amazing things that God has done and learning what the Body of Christ did to prepare for His moving in that special way. After hearing about revivals, the temptation is to simply try to do the exact same things on our campus. We recognize principles in scripture and in these stories that seem to be prerequisites to a great move of God, but we know we need to figure out what it looks like in our context. More important, we know that we cannot simply slap on a few new programs and expect transformation because campus transformation begins with personal renewal, a changing of the hearts of Christian students and campus ministers, not a change in programs. We'd also agree, however, that changes we make in our ministries and leadership can have profound effects on the hearts of students and ministries. So we recognize the value of learning from what God is doing in places that have experienced transformation, and we see the need to seek God for what we can learn and apply on our campus.

One of the things that got us moving toward this new model of campus ministry was watching the Sentinel Group's *Transformations* videos and reading books that told accounts of revivals around the world. We brought in speakers from some of these cities and nations to learn from them, to hear their stories, and to fuel our conversation and prayers toward UT. I think the myriad of teaching and perspectives we heard brought a depth to our vision and united our understanding of what we were trusting God to do at UT. Our understanding of what God was calling us to do in our context at UT was impacted most by the *Transformations* videos, by *City Reaching*, and by our subsequent conversations with Jim Herrington. In a sense, we were doing nothing more than what we saw and read in each of those resources, but we contextualized it to our campus.

Campus Reaching Defined

These few sentences in *City Reaching* really captured our imagination:

> *Imagine if the Body of Christ could unite around common infor-*
> *mation so that all are making decisions from the same set of facts.*
> *Each component has the same picture of the details, distinctions*
> *and distribution of the peoples and problems of the city. All having*
> *the same picture of the Body of Christ, its descriptions, distribu-*
> *tion, size and status. All seeing what is collectively being done and*
> *collectively what needs to be done. Each one determining the part*
> *they will play in reaching the whole* (City Reaching, pp. 64, 65).

This hope moved us forward. We wanted to see a campus where we all had the same complete picture, where each ministry determined its part of the whole. It seemed to us to be what the Body of Christ should look like on a campus. We took the defini-tion of "city reaching" given in the book and tweaked it a bit to reflect what we knew God was calling us to do together. After that, a new model of ministry at UT was born and embraced by most of the campus ministry leaders. I want to share our defini-tion and describe what it means to us. I hope that it will bring clarity to what we are doing and perhaps reveal how it is dif-ferent from attempts at unity that you may have experienced on your campuses.

Campus Reaching: *"The long-term, relational, and strategic process of partnering campus ministries in united prayer to build missional communities that transform the campus with the gospel of Jesus Christ."*

"LONG-TERM" - *Growing Persevering Leadership*

We recognize that transformation does not occur overnight. It means that we are committed to pray together and discover the vision over time, as God directs us. We know what we want to see. We're united around a vision, but we're aware that we do not know how to get there. We're also expectant that God will speak to us and lead us to specific next steps in His perfect time.

"RELATIONAL" - *Building Trusting Relationships*

Our relationships with one another as leaders are the basis for the whole process. We believe that the movement will never grow deeper than the depth of our personal relationships with one another. To partner together to the degree that campus reaching dictates, we have to have trusting relationships with one another. We can work together on an event or two without trust, but we cannot do campus reaching. Trust is crucial. Humility is equally important. We have to believe deep in our hearts that we need one another, that we have something to learn from one another, and that every ministry is needed and has something to add to the collective vision.

"STRATEGIC" - *Collaborating Beyond Events*

We're not just working together to sponsor random events or initiatives. Everything we choose to move forward in together is purposeful and fits into the larger campus-reaching vision. Ministry leaders are tired of working endlessly in committees to pull off an event often with little impact. We know this is not going to change our campuses. We know we need more united grassroots plans that connect students and build a prayer-based missional movement. We want to partner together in something that will last.

"Partnering" - *Sharing Gifts and Resources*

Every campus ministry that holds to historical orthodox Christianity is invited to participate. We believe that transformation will not come to our campuses until we're partnering our ministries together. Unity prepares the spiritual climate of the campus for transformation and allows us to get the best picture of what God and the enemy are doing so that we can determine the next steps forward in reaching the campus. We believe that every campus ministry has its own "redemptive gift," a unique way God has created that group to reach a specific part of the campus and to contribute to the collective campus-reaching vision. Therefore, we intentionally seek out leaders from every campus ministry, inviting them to join us in prayer and relationship.

"United Prayer" - *Mobilizing a Student Prayer Movement*

Prayer is where we begin, and prayer never stops. If we stop praying together across ministry lines on a weekly basis, then we stop campus reaching. Without prayer, we are just a committee working on events and projects. The first step in campus reaching is to unite ministry leaders in prayer on a weekly basis. It is in the place of prayer where vision and relationships grow, making the rest of the campus-reaching process possible. But prayer is not just for the leaders. A campus-wide prayer movement must grow as well. A united prayer movement must grow at every stage of the campus-reaching movement, creating the necessary breakthrough in the spiritual realm to prepare a campus for transformation.

"Missional Communities" - *Mobilizing a Student Missions Movement*

The tangible aim of campus reaching is to reach every people group on campus year after year, so that every student on campus would have a group of Christ-following friends living and sharing the gospel among them every day. We want to be ready to disciple the whole campus. In campus reaching, the campus is viewed as one large mission field. Ministries partner together to determine which people groups on campus are being reached and which are not in order to better partner and equip students to go to them. The goal in campus reaching is not to grow our ministries (though that will happen too). Rather, it is to equip and send our students to be ministers all over campus.

"TRANSFORMATION" - *Growing a Campus-wide Vision*

The goal is to see God glorified on campus in a historic way like we have read about in the past and observe around the world even now. We want to see thousands of students put their faith in Jesus. We want faculty to follow Jesus and teach their disciplines with a Christian worldview. We want to see students free from addictions and behaviors that harm them. We want students set free from depression and suicide. We want to see an end to unwanted pregnancies and abortions. We want a campus full of joy, peace, and community. We want to see our campuses become places that equip and send students as missionaries in the marketplaces of our cities and all over the world. This is the transformation we're seeking. This is the compelling vision that draws us together.

"THE GOSPEL OF JESUS CHRIST" - *Cultivating a Gospel-Centered Vision*

The good news of Jesus's death and resurrection for our redemption coupled with His lordship over us is the only thing that can bring transformation in us and on our campuses. The vision of a transformed campus is what brings us together in partnership, but we will never see the work of transformation apart the work of the gospel. The gospel is at the center of our vision. Our vision is rooted in a dependence on God's work in us and His message through us.

" I was skeptical. I had been a part of unity efforts before — all with good intentions but no lasting benefit to the Kingdom. But I was the new Baptist Student Ministry director for the UT campus and was feeling alone. So, I decided to go to the campus minister prayer meeting to meet some of my peers.

What I found on my first visit was a group of desperate campus ministers (like me) who were humbly seeking God for revival at the University of Texas, which at the time seemed to me to be a huge campus with few believers and darkness everywhere. This group wasn't planning "unity" events. They just worshipped together and prayed — with desperation.

Over the next few months I began to hear words like "campus transformation" and "campus reaching." Justin gave me a book called *City Reaching* and we watched the *Transformations* videos of incredible movements of God around the world. God began to plant in me the vision that He had already given this group: When the Body of Christ comes together in unified prayer — God moves! I began to truly believe God would transform the University of Texas.

In addition to praying together, we formed "covenant groups" of four to five campus ministers for personal accountability and connection. Most of our groups sounded like the beginning of a bad religious joke: "Did you hear the one about the Baptist, Methodist, Church of Christ, and Charismatic pastors?" We read books, drank coffee, laughed, and even cried together. These men and women became my closest brothers and sisters in Christ while at UT.

This unity was authentic — not symbolic. Deep — not surface. In a way, it ruined me. I have not looked at ministry or the Body of Christ the same since. "

JIMMY DANIEL
Baptist Student Ministry
CAMPUS MINISTER, 2000–2007

Campus-Reaching Strategies

We began defining campus reaching using the phrases described in the previous pages shortly after reading *City Reaching* and meeting with Jim Herrington. All of the words in the definition are meaningful to us, giving clarity to how this is different from attempts at unity that we had experienced in the past. If you have been on campus for very long, then I am sure you can see the difference we're talking about. Campus reaching is a new model of ministry, a way of pulling together the Body of Christ on campus to focus its gifts and resources on reaching the whole campus. If leaders are compelled by this vision and are willing to meet weekly to pray for transformation and build relationships with one another, then any campus can be on its way to discovering God's plan to reach every student on their campus with the gospel of Jesus.

Campus ministers at the University of Texas began praying into this vision in 1997. Soon thereafter, we sensed God leading us to move forward together in several common strategies. These simple practices arose out of our years of meeting with Jim Herrington. Now, four times a year, campus ministers at UT gather for several hours of planning — what we call Campus Minister Councils. Each time we look at these same five practices: Leadership Prayer Groups, Prayer Mobilization, Spiritual Mapping, Missional Communities, and Catalytic Events, and we ask, "What are the next steps to take?" in developing each of the five strategies. The second section of this book will explain these strategies and tell stories of what this process has looked like for us at UT. I hope it will inspire your imagination as you think about how the Body of Christ can work in partnership on your campus.

STRATEGIES for CAMPUS RENEWAL

leadership prayer groups (FUSION groups)

> **CAMPUS MINISTRY LEADERS PRAYING TOGETHER WEEKLY TO GROW IN RELATIONSHIP AND PARTNER IN MISSION FOR THE TRANSFORMATION OF A CAMPUS.**

In chapter 2, I described how we started gathering student leaders from each ministry to unite in prayer once a week. What I left out was the circumstances that caused us to do so. Our daily prayer group had been meeting for about a year, and we really desired to see our vision for transformation at UT caught by students from more ministries than just the few we represented. We figured that a large united worship and prayer gathering would be just the place to cast the vision.

It's hard to imagine, but this was back before students used the Internet! In order to find all of the Christian organizations at UT, we had to go to the student services building, flip open a gigantic book of the registered student organizations, and comb through it to find the Christian organizations. Each registered organization had to have three official student representatives. We called all of the representatives from the 30 campus ministries that did not have a student attending our daily prayer meeting and asked them to invite their ministries to join us for our first concert of prayer.

About 60 students attended the first concert of prayer, and all but five were from the five campus ministries represented at daily prayer. I remember being very discouraged by the turn-out, and I distinctly remember our "back to the drawing board experience" when we realized we should have first invited the leaders to weekly prayer instead of starting with a large event. We were expecting people who did not know us to invite their ministries to come to something we (whom they did not know) were leading. That night we began calling back these same ministry representatives and asking them if they would be willing to pray together once a week to get to know one another and to hear more about what God was doing through our various ministries.

By the end of the semester, about 20 of us were meeting weekly. At the end of one of our times of prayer, one of the students said, "Why don't we call all of our ministries together in a night of united worship and prayer for revival?" The next concert of prayer was attended by hundreds of students, and our vision for transformation spread to them.

College freshmen normally sleep in unless they have an 8 o'clock class, but my heart was longing to connect with other students who wanted to whole-heartedly follow Jesus. A very annoying alarm clock would go off at 6:45, giving me just enough time to slip out of the silent dormitory and walk across campus to the Student Union for morning prayer. I can remember the smell of the Lone Star room and the spot where we would huddle the sofa chairs together to approach God's throne together in reverence and with boldness.

Justin led us as we sought to know what was on God's heart. We were learning how to pray. We prayed for a greater refining work in our own lives, we carried each other's burdens, we lifted up the different ministries we were involved in, and we cried out for God to move on our campus, in our city, and throughout the world.

As things developed, Friday afternoons became the time when representatives from the different ministries on campus would join together in prayer. I can remember reading through John 17 together and thinking to myself, "Wow, we are actually getting to see what was on Jesus's heart when He prayed." The text came alive as God's Spirit was working in us — "I in them and you in me. May they be brought to complete unity to let the world know that you sent me and have loved them even as you have loved me" (John 17:23).

If you looked across the room and listened to how each person prayed, there was no doubt that we represented diverse groups, but there was a growing sense of being connected to something bigger. The Holy Spirit was working, bringing reconciliation, helping us to appreciate one another and calling us to something better.

Even though 15 years have gone by and I am now thousands of miles away as a missionary in Argentina, the desire to see Christ glorified through His unified Body still beats strong in my heart.

CHRISTOPHER YOUNG
Navigators
UT GRADUATE, 1998

Unlike the students, the campus ministers were reluctant to pray together. They thought that we were trying to get them to unite for unity's sake and that we'd function like some committee to work on united events. This was the depth of their experience of partnering together at that time. They thought we were proposing the same thing they had experienced before when a ministry wanted to partner for an event, and it was more about unity for unity's sake. It took the long conversations described in chapter 2 to create the clarity of vision needed for the ministers to begin to unite in prayer each week, and like the students, it was not long until they were sensing God's leading to something more. The key to starting a campus-reaching movement is starting a leadership prayer group for pastors and/or students so that relationships and vision can grow. Campus Renewal Ministries calls these leadership prayer groups Fusion Groups.

Fusion Groups

Fusion is defined as "the merging of different elements into a union." Fusion is when the best of two or more elements merge to make something even better.

On a Valentine's date a few years ago, I decided to take Brenda out to a fusion restaurant that a friend highly recommended. I had never heard of fusion food, so I went online to check it out (there was Internet by then). Their website read: "Nowhere else will you find a culinary experience quite like the flavors, textures, and colors found in Roy's Hawaiian Fusion Cuisine. Combining the freshest local ingredients with European sauces and bold Asian spices, each creation leaves you with the feeling that you've just found paradise." This fusion food combined the best local ingredients, the best European spices, and the best Asian spices. I remember having some sort of fish dish and thinking, "I have never tasted anything like this. It was the best of all flavors rolled into one."

This is what a Fusion Group is on a campus — a merging together of the leaders in the Body of Christ for weekly prayer so that, as relationships and vision grow, a new ministry model may emerge that blends the gifts of each campus ministry into one united movement. When this happens, ministry leaders will say, like I did, "I have never experienced anything like this. The best of all God's gifts rolled into one!"

The Body of Christ cannot partner in mission on campus unless the leaders of the ministries are first united in prayer. The campus-reaching process begins and ends with Fusion Groups. It's where relationships and vision grow, making the rest of the campus-reaching practices possible.

The Biblical Basis for United Leadership

In God's eyes, there is one church on our campus. All who confess the name of Jesus and have made Him Lord of their lives are part of God's family, the universal Church. "You are all sons of God through faith in Christ Jesus, for all of you who were baptized into Christ have clothed yourselves with Christ. There is neither Jew nor Greek, slave nor free, male nor female, for you are all one in Christ Jesus" (Gal. 3:26–28). Spiritually speaking, we are already one. Every Christian agrees with this, but we struggle knowing how to make what is true in the heavenly realm a reality here on earth.

I mentioned earlier during my first year of ministry how difficult it was trying to get the campus ministers to start a Fusion Group. One statement I often heard was, "We're already united in Christ. We don't need to pray together to be united." I always found this statement silly because we'd never apply the same argument to other areas of our lives. Brenda and I have been one in God's eyes since we were married on September 29, 2001. How would Brenda respond to me if she were trying to grow closer to me in our marriage and I said, "We're already one in God's eyes. Why do we need to spend more time together and grow more in love?" You can guess how she would respond! Similarly, we're already holy in God's eyes because of the sanctifying work of Jesus on our behalf. However, we're never told to simply sit on what is spiritually true. We're called to "walk out our salvation with fear and trembling" (Philippians 2:12) and to "offer our bodies as living sacrifices" (Romans 12:1).

In the same way, scripture makes clear that we are to "make every effort" to make what is true spiritually (our oneness in Christ) a living reality on our campuses. Paul encourages the church in Ephesus, "Be completely humble and gentle; be patient, bearing with one another in love. Make every effort to keep the unity of the Spirit through the bond of peace" (Ephesians 4:2–3). There is nothing passive about what he is asking the Church to do. After three chapters describing all that Christ did to make the Church one Body in God's eyes, he was now asking them to walk out their unity. Paul continues, asking them to use their unique gifts to "prepare God's people for works of service, so that the Body of Christ may be built up until we all reach unity in the faith and knowledge of the Son of God and become mature, attaining to the whole measure of the fullness of Christ" (Ephesians 4:12–13).

Ephesians is the premier biblical book on ecclesiology (the study of the Church), and it is a book calling us to practice our unity. God calls us to "make every effort" to be unified. He wants us to work as one Body to reach our campuses with the gospel of Jesus Christ. We need to "make every effort" because God asks us to do so, and our obedience honors Him. I believe God asks us to do so because He knows that when we are unified two things happen: The spiritual climate of our campus changes, and we are able to maximize our gifts and strengths.

Unity Changes the Spiritual Climate

While Ephesians is the premier book on ecclesiology, I Corinthians is a close second — mainly because the church was so dysfunctional! They were a church divided. They were getting drunk at the Lord's Supper and hindering others from partaking. They were having theological debates about meat sacrificed to idols. They were suing one another in court. They were getting divorces. They were using their spiritual gifts selfishly, their meetings were without order, and they were divided into different sects. In response to this, Paul gives one of the most difficult challenges in all of scripture: "I appeal to you, brothers, in the name of our Lord Jesus Christ, that you all agree with one another so that there may be no divisions among you and that you may be perfectly united in mind and thought" (I Corinthians 1:10). Agree with one another? That is the challenge? Really? How do you do that? I don't think it means we literally have to agree on every little thing. Later in chapter 8, Paul gives them freedom to disagree. I believe "agreeing" means that we humble ourselves before one another and continue in fellowship together by focusing on the essentials of the gospel and on our primary call to make disciples of every people group on our campus. Paul goes on to explain what happens in the spiritual realm when we refuse to agree with one another.

Division Stunts Our Growth

Paul told the Corinthians that he could only give them milk to drink, not solid food, because they were still infants in Christ. "For since there is jealousy and quarreling among you, are you not worldly? Are you not acting like mere men? For when one says, 'I follow Paul,' and another, 'I follow Apollos,' are you not mere men?" (I Corinthians 3:3–4). Their division was stunting their growth. Paul could not go deeper with the Corinthians because of their divisions.

In the same way, when we are not in partnership with one another, it affects the spiritual climate of our campus. God will not do a great work on our campuses as long as we are divided saying, "I'm a Crusader, Navigator, Methodist, Baptist, etc." Don't get me wrong, it's not about the words themselves. It is about our posture toward one another. Is there humility? Are we meeting together? Are we in the same room seeking God for the campus together? This is what it means to "agree with one another."

A few years ago, Gracepoint Community Church at the University of California at Berkley felt led to plant a church at UT. I met their pastor, Manny Kim, before he came to UT. He contacted me to find out more about the spiritual climate of the university. We had a great conversation, and I encouraged him to join our campus minister Fusion Group when he arrived in the fall. He joined us for prayer several times before coming to the Campus Minister Luncheon (which you will hear more about later in the book), where he was able to meet dozens of ministry leaders and hear about the ways we were partnering together. I spoke with him afterward and he said, "Wow. I did not know so much was happening. This is different from anything I have ever experienced at UC Berkley. We prayed together a few times a year, but this is clearly different." He witnessed that not only were we not in competition with one another, we derived our identities in Christ. We saw ourselves and other ministry leaders as first belonging to Christ and His Church, not our individual ministries.

At UT, we've grown to say something remarkable. We say, "Jesus is our senior pastor, and we're all associate pastors of His Church at UT." Again, it is not just the words. Many would assent to this truth, but are they committed to meeting and praying together to develop a vision of their campus together? If they are not, then they are stunting their growth.

" I distinctly remember Rez Week 2000, when the campus ministers were meeting with the Rez Week speaker David Bryant, from Concerts of Prayer International. He was describing the role of prayer during a revival he had experienced on campus when we was on staff with InterVarsity Christian Fellowship. Truthfully, I do not remember anything David said, but I remember very clearly what I sensed the Spirit was communicating with my heart.

I had been participating in the campus ministers' prayer time fairly regularly my first couple of years at UT. It had been very helpful, encouraging, and refreshing for me personally. Unity in the Body of Christ was a value to me, so I wanted to be a part when I had time. That morning, the Lord made it obvious to me that it was more valuable to Him than it had been to me and that I needed to make it more of a priority.

Specifically, I remember getting the message from God that my participation with the Body of Christ through the campus ministers' prayer time and the relationships and partnerships that I had with the other campus ministers and ministries was essential for the goals and dreams that I had been pursuing for the Texas Wesley campus ministry.

The Lord made it very obvious that this partnership, and specifically the prayer time together, was to be a high priority for me and a major building block to what He was doing in the campus ministry that I served. Since then, for the most part I have missed the campus ministers' prayer time only if I am out of town or have an emergency. It is permanently in my weekly schedule. This prayer time and the relationships and partnerships I have with other campus ministries have been a major part of how Christ has worked in and through the Texas Wesley. "

RUSTY TEETER
Texas Wesley United Methodist Campus Ministry
CAMPUS MINISTER, 1998–PRESENT

Division Ruins Our Witness

Paul was appalled at the fact that Corinthian believers were suing one another in court. He tells the Corinthians that this discredited their witness for Jesus, defeating them completely. "But instead, one brother goes to law against another — and this in front of unbelievers! The very fact that you have lawsuits among you means you have been completely defeated already. Why not rather be wronged? Why not rather be cheated?" (I Corinthians 6:6–7). What a convicting passage! Paul actually says it would be better to be wronged and forgive than to be hurt and divided.

Ask students on campus sometime why they are not connecting in a Christian community, and many will go on to describe how they are confused or disgusted at division in the Church or divisions among the Christian friends whom they know personally. If we are competing with one another, Paul says we have "already been completely defeated." Our very goal of discipling the whole campus is impossible if we're not doing it together. Simply put, the campus cannot be completely reached with the gospel unless we're in relationship pursuing this vision together.

The opposite, of course, is true in that unity enhances our witness. Jeremy Story relates a conversation he had during the first Rez Week when a student walked by and asked him, "Who is putting this on?" Jeremy explained that no single ministry was putting it on, but that this week all of the ministries canceled their normal meetings in order to come together as one united Body of believers. The guy was amazed and then asked Jeremy how he could begin to follow Jesus too. He put his faith in Jesus right there in the middle of campus. Jesus prayed, "May they be brought to complete unity to let the world know that you sent me and have loved them even as you have loved me" (John 17:23). Our unity is meant to be a powerful apologetic to the world around us. That night, during the first Rez Week, it obviously was to one student.

OUR VERY GOAL OF DISCIPLING THE WHOLE CAMPUS IS IMPOSSIBLE IF WE'RE NOT DOING IT TOGETHER. SIMPLY PUT, THE CAMPUS CANNOT BE COMPLETELY REACHED WITH THE GOSPEL UNLESS WE'RE IN RELATIONSHIP PURSUING THIS VISION TOGETHER.

Division Causes God to Resist Us

A common theological debate in the Corinthians' day was the topic of meat sacrificed to idols. Some believed Christians could eat this meat because everything was clean if it was received with thanksgiving. Others, however, thought it was not right. They believed that if they ate this meat, they would be participating in idolatry. Each side had a strong moral and theological argument. We would not have to think too hard to come up with several theological convictions where the Body of Christ disagrees today.

Although Paul had an opinion on the matter, he had a much larger point to make. "We know that we all possess knowledge. Knowledge puffs up, but love builds up. The man who thinks he knows something does not yet know as he ought to know. But the man who loves God is known by God" (I Corinthians 8:1–3). Paul cuts through the arguments. He says it is not about what they knew; it's about how they loved one another. The Corinthians were wrestling with the wrong question altogether. Instead of grappling with "Is it okay to eat meat sacrificed to idols?" they should have been wrestling with "How do we love and honor our brothers and sisters who believe differently than us?" This is a far more important question that demands our time and consideration.

The problem with knowledge is that it "puffs up," meaning it leads to pride, and God "resists the proud, but gives grace to the humble" (I Peter 5:5). Here is a very scary thought. If we have "knowledge pride" between one another in our campus ministries, God will resist us. With that in mind, it's about time we start asking better questions than those of predestination, tongues, baptism, healing, etc. It's time that we start asking, "How can we love and honor our brothers and sisters who believe differently than we do?" If we're not asking that question, then we will find ourselves fighting against God.

One of my favorite lunch meetings is my monthly get together with Mark Proeger, the pastor of Hope Student Life, and

John Newton, the priest at the Episcopal Student Center. Mark and John are great Christian thinkers, so our conversation always turns to some theological question or discussion on something we each view differently. John is an evangelical Episcopal minister, deeply committed to his denomination. Mark is an evangelical charismatic and his ministry actively seeks and practices supernatural spiritual gifts. I consider myself more of an evangelical that holds to a strange mix of charismatic and reformed viewpoints. So you can imagine that we have great conversations, each bringing a unique perspective to the table. At times, we find that we have more in common than anyone of us might think. Other times we see things differently. When we do have differing opinions, we don't waffle or hide our convictions. We share honestly, holding to our convictions and respecting each other's different perspectives. John and Mark are at our campus minister prayer meeting almost every week. Our vision for the campus and love for one another makes it easy to partner in ministry, no matter our subtle differences. The mission and our love for one another is much more important than what we think we know.

> **OUR VISION FOR THE CAMPUS AND LOVE FOR ONE ANOTHER MAKES IT EASY TO PARTNER IN MINISTRY, NO MATTER OUR SUBTLE DIFFERENCES. THE MISSION AND OUR LOVE FOR ONE ANOTHER IS MUCH MORE IMPORTANT THAN WHAT WE THINK WE KNOW.**

Unity Maximizes Our Gifts

We need unity on our campuses in order to see the spiritual climate change. This is most important, but there is a second reason to unite our ministries in one vision. When we do, we maximize our strengths. I Corinthians 12 is a wonderful passage about the Body of Christ. The body is a perfect analogy of how we're meant to work together. It details how we all have different "gifts," different "services," and different ways of "working" it out (I Corinthians 12:4–6). I take this to mean that on our campuses we have ministries with different spiritual gifts, different strategies, and different ministry philosophies.

By gifts, I mean some campus ministries may be gifted in teaching, while others are gifted in prayer, discipleship, evangelism, community, or prophecy. By strategies, I mean some campus ministries may have great outreach strategies, while others have great strategies for discipleship, worship, or missions. By ministry philosophies, I mean some campus ministries may have a philosophy that leads them to start missional communities, while others have a philosophy that leads them to create a powerful worship experience, seek social justice, start ethnic specific ministries, or multiply cell groups.

I Corinthians 12 teaches one thing: We all need each other. That's the point. Paul teaches that we cannot say, "I don't need you." Nor can we say, "I am not needed." In campus ministry, it is often the large churches and ministries that say to other campus ministries, "I do not need you." If they believe and act this way, then they are in sin and displeasing God. The smaller churches and campus ministries are the ones tempted to say to other campus ministries, "I am not needed." If they believe and act this way, then they are in sin and displeasing God. The truth is, we all need each other. Unity is God's revelation of our need for one another. We need one another, and this pleases God.

THE BIBLICAL TRUTH IS THAT WE DO NEED ONE ANOTHER. WE BELIEVE THAT LEADERS MUST ENTER INTO RELATIONSHIPS THROUGH PRAYER AND LET GOD GIVE THEM DIRECTION FOR HOW TO REACH THE CAMPUS TOGETHER.

At the University of Texas, as we have continued to meet together in prayer and conversation, ministries have grown to really know each other and recognize their need for one another. Those who are a hand in the Body of Christ now know the fingers, the wrists, the arms, and the shoulders. As a result, they have found ways to maximize their impact as the arm of the Body of Christ at UT. Those with similar gifts, ministries, and philosophies find ways to work together to maximize their impact, but it is not without the blessing and knowledge of the other parts of the Body of Christ. At least once a semester, we as the whole Body move into something greater together, and that is an incredible sight to see! The biblical truth is that we do need one another. We believe that leaders must enter into relationships through prayer and let God give them direction for how to reach the campus together.

BY MEETING WEEKLY TO PRAY, RELATIONSHIPS CAN GROW, AND GOD CAN SPEAK TO EVERYONE. THEN THE NEXT STEPS ARE REVEALED BY GOD TO THOSE WHO ARE PRAYING TOGETHER, AND THE GROUP CAN MOVE FORWARD WITH EVERYONE OWNING THE VISION, NOT JUST ONE MINISTRY.

I remember a unique moment many years ago when Morgan Stephens, the pastor for Every Nation Campus Ministries (ENCM), e-mailed me to set an appointment. Under his fantastic leadership, ENCM had grown rapidly, primarily by reaching lost students. I especially rejoiced in the way God was using their ministry to reach African American students. I met with Morgan once a semester just to hear what God was doing through their ministry and to encourage him to join the Fusion Group. However, he never joined us for prayer.

When Morgan e-mailed that he wanted to meet with me, I was happy that he initiated. When we got together, he told me that he had been at an ENCM conference the week before and heard one of their leaders give a message on unity using Psalm 133. He said he was convicted that he had not believed that he needed other ministries, nor had he believed that they needed him. Now, though, he planned to have all of his staff join us for prayer from that week forward. Over the last five or six years, I can hardly remember a time when the ENCM staff was not present at our Fusion Group. Morgan realized that in order to reach the whole campus, ENCM is needed, and that ENCM needs every other ministry at UT.

> One of my great joys as a pastor in Austin is seeing followers of Christ come together to accomplish something that none of us could accomplish individually. I have really enjoyed getting to spend time with others who want every student at UT to have a chance to respond to the gospel. The leaders of a vast array of ministries have spent hours together planning, praying, eating, and laughing. As we spend this time together planning united events, we've noticed that one of the benefits is the relationships that are being forged among us as leaders.
>
> The strength of these relationships was evidenced last year when my wife and I were blessed with the birth of our third baby boy. Our son was born at the beginning of the school year, which left me without anyone to lead our student leaders' retreat. So I turned to a few of the guys that lead other ministries here in Austin. The Campus Crusade director and a college pastor from another church stepped up and trained my students. I wasn't even at the training retreat, but I had no worries that our students were in good hands. I knew these men had tremendous character and that they shared my vision of equipping student leaders to reach students at UT. It's fun to be a part of a community of leaders who really see the big picture of God's vision for this campus. God's vision is bigger than any one of our ministries and to accomplish it will take us working together.

MATT BLACKWELL
Echo College Ministries, First Evangelical Free Church
CAMPUS MINISTER, 2005–PRESENT

Prayer Is the Starting Point

Prayer is the starting point for several reasons. It is the easiest way to unite. United prayer allows you to grow in relationship with one another. Uniting in prayer also cultivates vision and gives God an opportunity to give direction.

Many times we have seen ministry leaders try to move forward with a united plan without having prayed about it together beforehand. It either never gets underway or ends with discord. This is because leaders have underestimated the importance of relationships with one another and growing a united vision. Most often one ministry comes to the others with a specific event or a specific plan, but commitment is half-hearted because there is competition, and the leaders do not know one another personally. Before relationships are formed, ministry philosophies and even terminology can cause confusion, distrust, and resistance. Plus, in these situations, one ministry is taking the lead. The others are just following. They have not, through prayer, built relationships and heard from the Lord together as to the next steps they are to take. It is a completely different starting point.

Prayer is the place to start. By meeting weekly to pray, relationships can grow, and God can speak to everyone. Then the next steps are revealed by God to those who are praying together, and the group can move forward with everyone owning the vision, not just one ministry. This is very different from what most campus ministries have experienced in "uniting." If prayer is the starting point, the ending point is radically different!

" Today's world is competitive, independent, and often self-centered. Unfortunately, such influences often appear among the Body of Christ. Nonetheless, one may have difficulty finding Christian communities across the U.S. who enjoy the biblical unity that we have experienced at the University of Texas.

I am envious of newcomers to our UT campus ministry family. Seeking substantial fellowship with ministry leaders who share a common vision could not be much easier. New campus ministers are intentionally invited to our weekly prayer gatherings and warmly welcomed with prayers of thanksgiving and encouragement. This family atmosphere among campus ministries at UT has not always been so easy to find.

In 1988, I came as a Chi Alpha campus missionary to international students at UT. Few opportunities existed for interaction with other like-minded ministries, so years passed before I met fellow ministry leaders. In the late 1990s, Justin called campus ministry leaders to gather weekly for prayer. Few responded.

For years, we rejoiced on the occasions that our number climbed into double-digits.

Our weekly prayer connection planted genuine affection for each other. Over time, these seeds took root. Trust emerged along with an alertness to our common desire for the gospel of Jesus Christ to transform lives at the University of Texas. The fruitful flower of biblical unity had blossomed right before our eyes with little or no emphasis on events.

Sustaining our unity is challenged annually. The central values of connectedness in prayer and authentic relationship have been two critical components to this testimony. I am confident that the powerful promise of the psalmist will continue to be visible, "How good and how pleasant it is for brothers to dwell together in unity!...for there the LORD commanded the blessing..."(Psalm 133:1, 3 KJV).

KELLY BROWN
Chi Alpha Christian Fellowship
CAMPUS MINISTER, 1988–PRESENT

Tips for Fusion Groups

After leading student and minister Fusion Groups for almost 20 years now and having witnessed Fusion Groups on other campuses, I have found that there are several keys to leading a group successfully. Following these simple bits of advice will give a Fusion Group the best chance to thrive and move you forward into campus reaching.

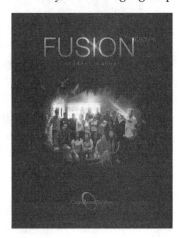

CRM has a Fusion Group Manual that can equip students or ministers to lead a Fusion Group. To help you cast vision for Fusion Groups on your campus, you can order or download a Fusion Manual and a weekly sample prayer guide from our website: www.campusrenewal.org.

Issue an Invitation Broadly

Invite ministry leaders to join you in prayer each week. Meet with leaders one on one, or call everyone to one larger gathering to share the vision and invite them to pray together. Begin with the leaders you know, but do not stop there. Contact ministry leaders you have not met yet. Go online to search for churches, college ministries, or registered student organizations. It is important to invite as many leaders as possible before you begin so that it does not appear that the group is exclusive. Also, if a Fusion Group is diverse from the beginning, new leaders are more likely to join you later.

In 1997, David Daniels, the college pastor of First Evangelical Free Church, helped me call all of the ministry leaders together. We sent them each a personal letter to join us for a conversation about unity and praying together. Issuing the invitation together with a few other people made a difference, as it was seen as something supported by several leaders, not just something Justin was trying to do again. We invited everyone, and about 25 leaders joined us for that first conversation. We started praying together the very next week.

Go with the Goers

Once an invitation has been extended, begin meeting with those who have expressed a desire to start a Fusion Group. Don't be discouraged if some are not yet ready to join you. Focus on those who are ready. Don't wait around for the most influential ministries to join you. The group is easier to join after it gets started. Once leaders begin to enjoy praying together, the word will get out, and others will make time to join the group.

We have had seasons when only 5 to 10 ministers were joining us every week, while the student Fusion Group had 20 to 30 people. At other times, we have struggled to get students committed to the Fusion Group, but ministers were faithfully attending. As you know, students and campus ministers come and go each year. The important thing is to stay faithful with a few and continue to call others to join you.

Pick a Time

Pick the day and time, and let others who are interested later adjust their schedules to make room to join you. As for the time, for ministers, we have found that late mornings often work best, giving those with families time to get their kids to school and those who have late night meetings the previous night a chance to sleep. Plus, in the morning, there is less chance of things popping up to pull ministers away. At UT, campus ministers meet on Wednesdays from 9 to 10 A.M. For students, we have found that late afternoons work best. Afternoons are less likely to conflict with classes, and they do not interfere directly with campus ministry meetings that many have in the evening. At UT, student leaders meet on Mondays from 5 to 6 P.M. The important thing is that you find a time that works for those who are committed to be a part of the Fusion Group.

Pick a Place

Pick a place that is best for everyone. If possible, in the beginning, don't meet at a particular ministry's location because that can give a sense that one ministry is leading the Fusion Group. That said, the group can be led in a way that makes it obvious to all that there is shared ownership. It's important to pick a place that is convenient for everyone, giving people a chance to get right back on campus afterward, so that the hour of prayer is not really a two-hour commitment. Find a place where there is parking and that is within walking distance from campus. We suggest not moving locations throughout the year, as it can just cause confusion and more need for communication. Over the years at UT, we have met outdoors on campus, at the First Evangelical Free Church, at the Baptist Student Ministry, at Hope Chapel, and now we meet more permanently at the Campus House of Prayer.

Meet Weekly

We have found that groups that do not meet weekly are never able to move forward into the campus-reaching vision. You know this to be true too. Just as your own campus ministries call leaders to meet weekly in order to grow in vision and relationships, so too Fusion Groups need to meet weekly. Meeting once a month or meeting every other week is not enough face time to begin campus reaching.

Twice a semester we cancel the prayer meeting and have what we call the Campus Minister Council, which is a lengthy meeting for planning and conversation. Every now and then someone comes to the Campus Minister Council whom we have not seen at prayer all semester. It is more difficult for that person to contribute because others do not know him, nor has he been praying into the vision with everyone each week. Those who do see each other every week have the most to contribute because they have shared life and ministry for months prior to our strategic council meeting.

Leading Prayer

If the time of prayer is not led well, the Fusion Group will not fulfill its purpose of helping leaders grow in their relationships with one another and their vision for the campus. We have found that Fusion Groups do best when they focus on three things: God, the campus, and each other. To help focus your prayers on these three topics, CRM has created a sample prayer guide that gives scriptures and points of prayer for each week of the semester that you meet. The prayer guide can be found on our website: www.campusrenewal.org.

Focus on God. He is the reason you are meeting together, so spending time in worship (music or spoken prayers of thanksgiving and praise) focuses the group like nothing else can. Each time of prayer should include time spent in worship.

Focus on the campus. Use scripture to guide prayers for campus transformation. Don't merely share what each ministry is doing and pray for the ministries. The purpose of a Fusion Group is to begin to dream of something beyond your individual ministries, so make a point to pray beyond them. Pray for the lost and for unreached people groups. Pray for unity, humility, repentance, and a hunger for God. Corporately confess sin in the Body of Christ and the campus at large. Imagine a transformed campus, and pray for God to do something historic in your day!

Focus on each other. Pray for each other. Share personal prayer requests and prayer requests for your ministries. This is where relationships can grow as you drop your guard, admitting your need for each other. Keep sharing time brief so that you can get to prayer, but make room to minister to one another.

Depending on the size of your group, it may be helpful to break into smaller groups at some point during the hour. Always spend some time in a large group, no matter the size, as it is important to pray together and hear each other's hearts expressed through prayer.

Finally, it's helpful to switch leaders from week to week. This is a great way to get to know one another, and it communicates that this is a united prayer gathering. Have a different person lead worship each week or so. Have a different person share a scripture and direct the prayer. Switching leaders is not necessary though. What is most important is that someone comes prepared to lead. Someone needs to give attention each week to leading the Fusion Group's focus on God, the campus, and each other.

WHAT IS MOST IMPORTANT IS THAT SOMEONE COMES PREPARED TO LEAD. SOMEONE NEEDS TO GIVE ATTENTION EACH WEEK TO LEADING THE FUSION GROUP'S FOCUS ON GOD, THE CAMPUS, AND EACH OTHER.

Setting Some Ground Rules

It may not be necessary, but often having some ground rules can be beneficial. It can disarm those who have had a negative experience with similar gatherings. When we began our Fusion Group, we set a few rules. We asked that no one come with fliers or announcements. We asked for no "theological posturing" in prayer and no "preaching prayers" (you know what I am talking about). We asked for prayer requests to be shared briefly, so that we could actually do what we came to do: Pray. We asked that everyone arrive on time, and we promised to end on time. Finally, we agreed to have the strictest confidentiality, giving people freedom to share about personal struggles or issues within their ministries. These common agreements made the Fusion Group a safe place where we could grow to really know one another and pray for God to move beyond the scope of our individual ministries.

The Beauty of the United Body of Christ

The psalmist is right when he says, "How good and pleasant it is when brothers dwell together in unity" (Psalm 133:1). Fusion Groups are really special. They are the first step to "merging different elements into one." Campus reaching cannot begin until a Fusion Group is born, for it is in the place of prayer that we grow to trust one another and God reveals His plans. "There the LORD bestows His blessing" (Psalm 133:3).

Several Fusion Groups stick out in my memory over the years. I remember a time when a campus minister "interrupted" prayer, saying that he needed prayer because he was struggling with depression. His honesty and brokenness opened up a new level of relationship within the group. In the following weeks, ministers began to share about their struggles in their marriages, feelings of incompetency, even confessing comparing themselves with others in the room. Those were important weeks in developing a new level of love and trust.

I remember a time when a pastor whom I never thought would visit us joined our group. At the end of our time we broke into smaller groups to pray for personal needs. The pastor later told me that when the two women from Campus Crusade laid hands on him to pray, it was the first time he had ever received prayer from any minister, including within his denomination! He left a changed man with a new call on life. A year later he left his difficult position as college pastor with his church and became a missions pastor in Austin at a wonderful fellowship within his same denomination.

In 1994, a few years after we started the student Fusion Group, several of the students from the Texas Wesley United Methodist campus ministry began asking us to pray for their ministry to call an evangelical minister to their vacant position. We prayed every week with them, and a year later they were blessed with a wonderful evangelical minister named Rusty Teeter. Under his leadership the Texas Wesley is once again making an impact on campus, and Rusty is one of the ministers most deeply committed to the campus-reaching movement.

I also remember a time two years ago when God simply took over the student Fusion Group and the campus minister Fusion Group. There is no other way to describe it than that. I had a plan and a direction for leading the group time, but early on as we worshipped and prayed, it was obvious that God had something different in mind. The ministers' Fusion Group spent an hour spontaneously reading and praying scriptures about Jesus and worshipping him. The student Fusion Group just never stopped worshipping. We sang songs together and burst into spontaneous songs of worship for the entire hour. It's times like these that you see and feel the beauty of the Body of Christ.

❝ **Leading, and even just being a part of the Fusion Group, is one of my favorite things about college. The sweetness, tenderness, and joyful excitement of God seems to join us every time** we come together, and I truly have a sense that we are changing the spiritual fabric of the campus through our prayer.

Over the past two years, we have seen Jesus move with increasing power and deeper love on campus, and I believe united prayer has been one of the foundational reasons for the Body of Christ's earnest participation with God. Our prayer is helping knit the Church at UT together so that the Body of Christ can walk effectively on campus.

It has been great to unite students in prayer each week. We really get a sense of God's perspective of the whole campus, and we gain insight into how He's bringing light into the rest of the university. We praise God together when we share brief testimonies about what God is doing in each of our ministries. We share the praises and prayer concerns of the ministries. It is wonderful to see that, instead of being jealous or judgmental, we can grow in humility, unity, and genuine love toward each other. We have grown to believe that we are not distant relatives with a common ancestry and different traditions. Instead, we are unique, but equally lovely, children of the same Father. 🎵🎵

JILL BAGGERMAN
Campus Renewal Ministries
UT STUDENT, CLASS OF 2012

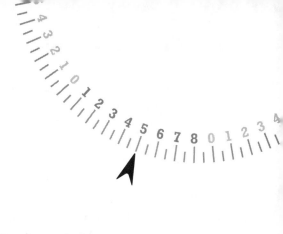

PRAYER
mobilization

> ❝ MOBILIZING THE BODY OF CHRIST TO SEEK GOD FOR THE TRANSFORMATION OF THE CAMPUS THROUGH UNITED PRAYER AND FASTING. ❞

As I look back upon my years as a student, like many people, I see them as some of the best years of my life. Almost all of my closest friends and brothers in Christ I met while I was a student at the University of Texas. In fact, 15 years after graduation, a number of us still meet twice a year at a lake house for the summer's fantasy football draft and the spring "owners meetings" (read: an excuse to play poker). One of the guys, Stephen, always comes to the retreats with a specially made game show in which all of the questions and answers are about our days together at UT! It is hilarious. Thankfully, we're still young enough to remember some of the answers!

When I think back on my years at college, my fondest memory is of our daily prayer group. It's hard for me to believe that a group of friends and I prayed together from 7 to 8 A.M. every day that there were classes, for four years. You can imagine how close we became and how our vision was united through prayer. In addition to praying scriptural prayers for revival every day before class, we also began reading books about revival that built our faith. Dan Hayes's book, *Fireseeds of Spiritual Awakening*, describes how most awakenings start with a small group of students praying, then that group calls others to pray, and a movement of prayer begins. Challenged by the book, we began calling the whole campus to prayer, beginning with the student Fusion Group and moving from there to concerts of prayer, then to a 168-hour prayer chain, then to "prayer saturation" strategies where at different times we were praying by name for all 3,000 UT professors and all 8,000 UT freshmen.

We experienced how God was changing us as we prayed. He was giving us compassion for our unbelieving friends, giving us purity as we confessed sin, and giving us faith as we prayed for God to do something that only He could do. We wanted the rest of the Body of Christ to believe with us that God could make His name great on our campus. For us, it started with prayer. So we knew we had to invite others into prayer as well.

The Biblical Basis for Prayer Mobilization

Prayer Always Precedes Revival

Revival is always preceded by a growing movement of prayer. It is the clear pattern seen historically and biblically. The pattern is set in Judges and seen throughout scripture: God's people sin, God brings judgment upon them, God's people confess their sins and cry out in prayer, and God responds by bringing renewal. This pattern is seen repeatedly throughout the period of the kings of Israel and Judah when times of awakening preceded by prayer were led by such kings as Asa, Jehoshaphat, Hezekiah, and Josiah. Samuel, Nehemiah, and Ezra were all leaders God used to lead their people in prayer and repentance, resulting in awakening. The prophets called for it throughout scripture, many echoing the words of Hosea and Joel:

> *Then I will go back to my place until they admit their guilt. And they will seek my face; in their misery they will earnestly seek me. Come, let us return to the* Lord. *He has torn us to pieces but he will heal us; he has injured us but he will bind up our wounds. After two days he will revive us; on the third day he will restore us, that we may live in his presence. Let us acknowledge the* Lord; *let us press on to acknowledge him. As surely as the sun rises, he will appear; he will come to us like the winter rains, like the spring rains that water the earth* (Hosea 5:15–6:3).

> *"Even now," declares the* Lord, *"return to me with all your heart, with fasting and weeping and mourning." Rend your heart and not your garments. Return to the* Lord *your God, for he is gracious and compassionate, slow to anger and abounding in love, and he relents from sending calamity. Who knows? He may turn and have pity and leave behind a blessing — grain offerings and drink offerings for the* Lord *your God. Blow the trumpet in Zion, declare a holy fast, call a sacred assembly. Gather the people, consecrate the assembly; bring together the elders, gather the children, those nursing at the breast. Let the bridegroom leave his room and the bride her chamber. Let the priests, who minister before the* Lord, *weep between the temple porch and the altar. Let them say, "Spare your people, O* Lord. *Do not make your inheritance an object of scorn, a byword among the nations. Why should they say among the peoples, 'Where is their God?'"* (Joel 2:12–17).

Even the birth of the Church at Pentecost was preceded by prayer, as the followers of Jesus were in the upper room praying before the Holy Spirit filled them. They continued to pray together every day, and the gospel advanced through their united prayers. "After they prayed, the place where they were meeting was shaken. And they were all filled with the Holy Spirit and spoke the word of God boldly" (Acts 4:31).

Scripture sets the precedent through both stories and commands. Prayer always precedes revival. This can be seen in extra-biblical history as well. These extra-biblical stories were the ones that first captured my heart and imagination. I remember hearing about Samuel Mills at Williams College in Massachusetts. In 1806, he and some friends had begun meeting to pray for the nations and to dream about how they could mobilize students to go out as missionaries. The group called themselves the Society of Brethren. Though they began as a secret society on campus, many more joined their prayer movement, and student groups from other campuses took on the same name and purpose. Soon revival broke out on campuses across America. Within a few years, they had formed the first missions-sending agency in the history of our country. Samuel Mills and the Society of Brethren had a huge impact on another group of students 80 years later who gathered in 1886 at the Mt. Hermon Conference of college students. A small group of students were praying for revival, asking specifically for God to renew in students a heart for the nations. The last night of the conference, July 24, 1886, God showed up and 100 students committed themselves, God willing, to go to the foreign mission field. Students left the conference and began to travel to campuses, sharing their vision for

PRAYER IS, AFTER ALL, A SIGNIFICANT WAY TO MEASURE OUR HUNGER FOR GOD AND THE SIZE OF OUR VISION. IF WE'RE TRUSTING GOD TO DO SOMETHING BIGGER THAN WE COULD POSSIBLY DO OURSELVES, THEN WE'RE GOING TO HAVE TO PRAY.

revival and world missions. Thus began the Student Volunteer Movement, the largest missions-sending movement in our country's history, sending more than 20,000 graduates overseas.

These stories began in prayer, as did the First and Second Great Awakenings, the Laymen's Prayer Movement, the Welsh Revival, and the stories being written today — like the stories of Almolonga, Guatamala; Cali, Colombia; Fiji Islands; and Kampala, Uganda — that are documented in the Sentinel Group's *Transformations* videos. There is never awakening without a growing prayer movement. In fact, it could be argued that prayer is revival. Prayer is, after all, a significant way to measure our hunger for God and the size of our vision. If we're trusting God to do something bigger than we could possibly do ourselves, then we're going to have to pray. If we want more of God than what we currently experience, then we need to pray. When students get up early or stay up late to seek God together, when hundreds are coming to united gatherings to pray and repent, when ministry leaders are setting aside time to meet once a week or more, when many students are fasting from food and entertainment, then we will know that revival is coming. It may already be here.

" Freshman year, 1994, I had my first experience participating in a campus-wide concert of prayer. I played bass for the assembled band consisting of musicians from varying campus ministries and churches. I had hopes, but not high expectations, about how believers across denominational lines, each with their own preferences and prejudices concerning worship styles, would respond to each other. After all, some of the campus ministries did not seem to like each other much, judging by their independence from each other at other times of the year and some of the known rivalries which existed among groups. Nonetheless, we counted on the fact that our band of talented musicians and worship leaders could help facilitate some semblance of unity through the worship music. Or so we thought.

Midway through the first song, we had a power outage. Our hearts sank. Looking back, I see the Lord's handiwork and wisdom in taking our band out of the picture, so that we could be quiet enough to attend to what the Spirit of God was doing. Standing outside in the dark, strangers laid aside their prejudices, joined hands with one another, confessed sins corporately, and cried out to God to heal and revive our land. There is no way to explain the unity that was experienced that night except that it was an outpouring of the Spirit. There was no "concert" effect thanks to the blackout. It was simply the Spirit manifesting Himself among us, as we gathered to pray in one accord. We left that evening with a sense of awe and anticipation for a coming revival on the UT campus. 🙿

DAVID WU
Chinese Bible Study
UT GRADUATE, 1998

Prayer Changes Us

This is God's secret agenda in prayer: to change us. That's why, in one sense, prayer is revival. When the Body of Christ is seeking God in prayer, it is sure to bring transformation, and a revived church is the first step to a revived campus. Transformation starts with us.

When I was a new believer, I remember being encouraged to pray daily for a number of friends who were not following Jesus. I thought, naturally, of some of the guys on my high school football team. Many of these friends were part of the group I hung out with before I gave my life to Jesus. Truthfully, I had some anger at them for the way they treated me. I was that kid who allowed people to pick on me so long as I could still be part of the group. Something funny happened, however, as I began to pray for these guys each day. My heart for them changed. My bitterness turned to compassion, by doing nothing more than praying for them daily. God's secret purpose in prayer was accomplished. I was changed.

Jesus taught us, "Love your enemies, do good to those who hate you, bless those who curse you, pray for those who mistreat you" (Luke 6:27–28). He knew that doing good, blessing, and praying for those who are against us would actually change our hearts toward them, making it possible to love them. This is the purpose of prayer, to change us. The more we pray for the lost, the more our compassion grows, which makes us pray more, and the cycle continues.

Paul said, "Do not be anxious about anything, but in everything, by prayer and petition, with thanksgiving, present your requests to God. And the peace of God, which transcends understanding, will guard your hearts and minds in Christ Jesus" (Philippians 4:6–7). He knew that prayer and thanksgiving could change our hearts. The more we spend time praying prayers of thanksgiving for all God has given us, the more grateful we become, which makes us want to thank God more.

We need to build united movements of prayer on our campuses, because when we do, God will transform the lives of those praying. Campus revival begins with the transformation of the believer. As we pray, we are changed. Transformation never comes to a campus when there is no hunger for God, no vision for something beyond the current reality, and no brokenness over sin. Hunger, vision, and brokenness are cultivated (if not measured) by our prayer lives. When we are broken over sin (personal sin and corporate sin), we spend time in confession, which cultivates more brokenness. When we are hungry for more of God, we seek Him in prayer, which cultivates more hunger. When we seek a campus-wide vision, we must pray beyond ourselves, which cultivates more vision. Prayer is revival, which is why the campus-reaching vision for transformation begins by mobilizing prayer.

THIS IS GOD'S SECRET AGENDA IN PRAYER: TO CHANGE US. THAT'S WHY, IN ONE SENSE, PRAYER IS REVIVAL.

For the last several years, CRM has held a retreat for UT students during Christmas break. We call it the "Revival Retreat," because we study the topic of revival for several days. Every student is required to read three books in order to attend the retreat. We have read different books each of the three years we have held the retreat. Every year one book is a history book, one is a theology book, and the other is a practice/principles book. It is inspiring to get so many thoughtful students together for several days to worship, pray, and have conversations about revival. I expected it to help develop leaders, but I had no idea how it would really change students' lives.

A few years ago I had a trusted friend come spend a week with me at UT to observe our work, interview ministers and students, and ultimately to consult with me about ways to improve my leadership. I was present during one of the sessions he held with students. He asked the students to describe turning points in their lives at UT as they intersected with our ministry. Rez Week and the Revival Retreat were listed by almost everyone. They said that being part of 24/7 prayer on campus during Rez Week and our lengthy times of prayer during the Revival Retreat changed their lives. Note: They said the time we spent in prayer changed them, not the books, my teaching, or the messages given at Rez Week. It was simply meeting with God and others in the place of prayer that God used to make them more like Himself.

Prayer Wins the Spiritual Battle

Our campuses cannot be transformed by our unified strategies, no matter how strategic our plans may be, because the battle for the hearts of students is a spiritual battle. There is no conviction of sin, desire for God, or illumination of God's word without the work of the Holy Spirit in an individual's life. Paul reminds us, "The god of this age has blinded the mind of unbelievers, so that they cannot see the light of the gospel of the glory of Christ, who is the image of God" (II Corinthians 4:4). Therefore, we must pray, asking God to do what only He can do — change hearts.

If we want to see God move on our campuses, we cannot spend the bulk of our time in planning, strategizing, and talking.

Our plans are always going to fail, apart from the mighty work of the Holy Spirit who is invited to do what only He can do as we unite in prayer. In fact, when prayer is made the first priority, we're more likely to hear from God and develop strategies that the Holy Spirit has given us as we have prayed.

In II Corinthians Paul is defending his ministry to the Corinthians who had been enticed to follow men who practiced worldly forms of authority. They followed these men because of their fear tactics, spiritual experiences, false but authoritative teaching, and the titles they gave themselves. Throughout the letter, Paul claims that he does not rely on worldly tactics, but on the Holy Spirit, because the battle for people's lives and souls is a spiritual battle. He says, "The weapons we fight with are not the weapons of the world. On the contrary, they have divine power to demolish strongholds. We demolish strongholds and every pretension that sets itself up against the knowledge of God, and we take captive every thought to make it obedient to Christ" (II Corinthians 10:4–5). On our campuses we're fighting strongholds and the thoughts of the enemy, such as relativism, pluralism, hedonism, fatherlessness, entertainment, lust, boredom, depression, busyness, materialism, greed, fear, etc. Do we really think our best strategies and plans can make a bit of a difference against such thoughts and strongholds? Not without God. We need Him to show up, so we need to pray.

During my junior year at UT, I remember being confused and aggravated by a professor in my philosophy class. He was deceiving the class with some of his teaching,

IF WE WANT TO SEE GOD MOVE ON OUR CAMPUSES, WE CANNOT SPEND THE BULK OF OUR TIME IN PLANNING, STRATEGIZING, AND TALKING. OUR PLANS ARE ALWAYS GOING TO FAIL, APART FROM THE MIGHTY WORK OF THE HOLY SPIRIT WHO IS INVITED TO DO WHAT ONLY HE CAN DO AS WE UNITE IN PRAYER.

and I was frustrated with my inability to communicate my disagreements. After class, I walked out to one of the lawns on campus and began to get down on myself for not being smart enough to challenge the professor.

WE CAN'T MAKE PLANS, AND THEN PRAY FOR GOD TO BLESS OUR PLANS. THAT'S THE WRONG ORDER. WE SHOULD DEVELOP MOVEMENTS OF PRAYER THAT ARE BIGGER THAN OUR PLANS.

God quietly reminded me that the battle for my professor and classmates was spiritual, and they were not going to believe the truth because of anything I could ask or say. I did not use this as an excuse not to continue to seek answers, but I used the encouragement to pray for my professor and classmates more than looking for ways to communicate truth to them.

We can't make plans, and then pray for God to bless our plans. That's the wrong order. We should develop movements of prayer that are bigger than our plans. We need to seek God together and let our plans come from God as we listen to Him in prayer. Prayer is where we must begin. "For our struggle is not against flesh and blood, but against the rulers, against the authorities, against the powers of this dark world, and against the spiritual forces of evil in the heavenly realm. Therefore put on the full armor of God, so that when the day of evil comes, you may be able to stand your ground, and after you have done everything, to stand. And pray in the Spirit on all occasions with all kinds of prayers and requests. With this in mind, be alert and always keep praying for all the saints" (Ephesians 6:12–13, 18).

For Rez Week in 2001, we wanted to place a tent in the middle of campus for 24/7 prayer. UT's administration had many concerns, however, and pushed back on the idea. A week before Rez Week we were still unsure if we were going to be granted permission. I was prepared to start calling lawyers and other high-ranking officials whom I hoped could sway the university's opinion. At the campus ministers' Fusion Group that week, I expressed my frustration to the ministers, and we began to pray for God to change the administration's heart. In the middle of our prayers, Kelly Brown from Chi Alpha interrupted to suggest that we pray blessings over the administration, given that the battle was spiritual, not physical. The atmosphere of the Fusion Group changed in a very healthy way. An hour later I received the call from UT that our plans were approved. The battle was spiritual, and God simply won over the hearts of the administration as we blessed them in prayer.

    As a freshman at the University of Texas, God began to stir my heart for revival. It was a clear moment in my dorm room where I heard the Holy Spirit speak to me, "Do you believe I can save all 50,000 students?" My spirit responded positively in faith, and so began my journey to find like-minded people to believe for something great.

I remember hearing about a Campus Renewal Ministries prayer meeting to pray for UT and knew I needed to attend. At this meeting, students from different ministries came together to pray weekly for the campus — that revival would come and shake the hearts of lost students. From this group, a leadership team was formed to plan and develop our annual Rez Week celebration.

As we met and prayed together, we studied the history of our campus and different revivals that were happening across the world. In every situation, prayer was the catalyst for these spiritual movements. As students we were desperate to see God move on our campus, and we knew it would take more than a prayer meeting.

The leadership team decided to lead the first 24/7 prayer initiative during Rez Week in the spring of 2001. The excitement and team unity was really significant. From there we began to see a deeper hunger from students to pray on a more regular basis. It didn't matter what ministry you were a part of, students just had a heart to meet and pray for God to move in big ways.

As a minister on the UT campus for the last seven years, I have only seen the passion for prayer deepen and grow. Without first petitioning God in prayer, I can't imagine what the spiritual climate of our campus would be. **"**

KRISTIN EDWARDS
Every Nation Campus Ministry
CAMPUS MINISTER, 2003–PRESENT

How to Mobilize Prayer

The first step in mobilizing prayer is to start a Fusion Group. The previous chapter described this in detail, but it bears mentioning again here. It is impossible to begin campus-wide prayer mobilization strategies before leaders of campus ministries are in trusting relationships with one another. An outsider coming to individual ministries asking them to do something together just doesn't work. If, however, leaders are praying together each week, and God speaks to the whole group, or even one or two people in the group, about a specific way to mobilize prayer, then the leaders will be much more willing to unite their ministries in prayer. Begin by starting a Fusion Group, then attempt prayer mobilization events before finally moving on to more long-term prayer mobilization strategies.

Prayer Mobilization Events

Simple one-night events can be used to spur on a movement of prayer by teaching people how to pray, by casting vision, and by initiating prayer mobilization strategies. Giving students an experience of prayer that demystifies it by teaching them how to pray simple prayers for the campus can ignite a movement of prayer. Large events can also be a great place to cast a campus-wide vision, so that students from multiple ministries can begin to imagine what it could look like to work as one Body of Christ to see their campus transformed by the gospel of Jesus. When your campus is ready to attempt prayer mobilization strategies, the events can be used to launch the strategies. Although there are many possibilities for prayer mobilization events, we suggest starting with concerts of prayer and prayerwalking.

Concerts of Prayer

One of the first things we started doing at the University of Texas was leading concerts of prayer once or twice a semester. A concert of prayer, which we have also called All Campus Worship or a Sacred Assembly in the past, is simply a night of united worship and prayer. Notice I said worship and prayer, not teaching. Concerts of prayer are different from a typical worship service or your normal large group gatherings. They have an ebb and flow of different types of prayer and songs that fit with the direction of the prayer so that we can sing a united prayer before moving on to the next season of prayer.

Concerts of prayer are meant to be fast-paced so that the students who would be hesitant about praying for two hours will end the night surprised at how easy it was to pray with others and how fast the two hours flew by. Many students and ministers come on stage to lead prayer in a specific direction by reading scripture, telling the audience how to pray (both what to pray and what size groups to form), and by praying an example opening prayer before everyone prays in their groups.

BEGIN BY STARTING A FUSION GROUP, THEN ATTEMPT PRAYER MOBILIZATION EVENTS BEFORE FINALLY MOVING ON TO MORE LONG-TERM PRAYER MOBILIZATION STRATEGIES.

Below is the schedule we used for our concert of prayer during Rez Week 2010. We had Matt Chandler, a well-known speaker and pastor of the Village Church in Flower Mound, Texas, with us for the three nights prior to this concert of prayer. About 700 students showed up each night to worship and hear Matt teach. Truthfully, we expected far fewer students to show up for the concert of prayer, particularly because we asked everyone to fast that day and Matt would no longer be with us. We were surprised to see 500 students join us for two hours of prayer and confession led by students and a few ministers. It was one of the most powerful times of repentance that we have ever had at Rez Week.

Rez Week 2010 Concert of Prayer

7:10 - Worship *(3 upbeat songs welcoming God)*

7:20 - Introduction and Opening Prayers
- Explain what a Solemn Assembly is (Joel 2)
- Explain how tonight will work

7:35 - Identificational Repentance
- Explain "Korean style" prayer (When we all pray aloud at the same time)
- Students lead specific prayers of repentance using scripture and praying an example prayer. Afterward students pray repentance prayers Korean style.
  - *Academics/Busyness*
  - *Judging/Unloving*
  - *Entertainment/Distractions*
  - *Pride/Self-Worship*
  - *Apathy/Compassionlessness*
  - *Addictions/Idolatry*
  - *False Worship/Hypocrisy*
  - *Materialism/Selfishness*
  - *Self-Reliance*

7:50 - Worship *(1 song of repentance)*

7:55 - Ethnic Reconciliation
- Students explain how they have been hurt by racism
- Break into interracial groups of 3–4
- Prayers of repentance

8:10 - Gender Repentance
- Break up into same gender guys and girls groups of 6–8
- Male and female students confess their gender-specific sins and pray prayers of repentance

- Blessing prayer (face the opposite gender and pray Korean style blessing for the opposite gender)

8:25 - WORSHIP *(1 song of repentance)*

8:30 - DENOMINATIONAL REPENTANCE

- Explanation of the three "streams" through which campus ministries see transformations: Justice, Salvation, and Miracles
- Break into groups with people from different campus ministries
- Campus minister representing each stream prays an example prayer of confession for their stream

8:50 - WORSHIP *(3 songs of joy and praise to God)*

9:00 - CLOSING PRAYER AND BLESSING

Prayerwalking

Another great prayer event is a prayerwalk. Prayerwalking is nothing more than praying aloud while you walk around campus. It's not meant to be a demonstration of any sort. Rather, groups of two or three walk together on a specific route and pray for the campus according to what they see and hear. My friend Steve Hawthorne, author of *Prayer-Walking*, says it's "praying on the scene without making one." Prayerwalking teams pray for the dorms and the lecture halls they pass. They pray for the sports teams as they walk by school stadiums. They pray prayers of repentance for things they overhear and see. They pray the scriptures over quotations they see on buildings and statues around campus.

Prayerwalks can be organized many ways. A group of 100 students can prayerwalk the same route, forming what looks like a marching line of fifty groups of two, or groups can walk many different routes starting and ending at the same point. We have found it especially helpful to send students out on various routes, organizing them across ministry lines to prayerwalk their specific departments or residences, and then have them return to one place to share about what they prayed and what they learned. This provides them an opportunity to meet other believers who live in their part of campus and/or are studying in the same departments. We'll discuss this further in the chapter on missional communities, but this also helps them see how God could use them to reach their residence or department. Prayerwalking opens students' eyes to things they see every day, but often without spiritual eyes. It changes the way they walk through their day, making them more aware of the people around them. It is an event that fosters more prayer as a result. Often those who prayerwalk specific departments decide to meet again to pray for their classmates and friends at a future time.

One of my favorite prayerwalking experiences was joining a group of students who prayerwalked the perimeter of UT every day during spring break. The last day they did a "Jericho Walk," where they walked around the campus seven times from midnight to 7 A.M. I joined them for the last lap, and it was incredible. After days of walking they had identified specific things to pray for. Their prayers were full of insight and hope, and yes, we ended the walk with a very loud yell asking God to break down the spiritual walls hindering God's work at UT.

Prayer Mobilization Strategies

Events are important to teach students how to pray and to cast vision for the campus, but prayer is better mobilized when campuswide strategies are developed that get students praying on their own, in their small groups, in their classes and dorms, and in campus ministries. The Body of Christ on campus can only come together in prayer events once or twice a semester, but prayer strategies can be implemented to empower each campus ministry and small groups of students to be united in prayer without ever meeting together. A grassroots, multiplying movement of prayer is what precedes revival. This is the type of prayer we need to mobilize on our campuses. Beyond prayer events, there are many

other possible prayer strategies that you can implement on your campus. To help you think about possibilities on your campus, I have classified these strategies into three categories: focused prayer, saturation prayer, and continuous prayer.

Focused Prayer

Focused prayer strategies are those that unite the body in praying specific things for the campus. Focused prayers don't bring the Body together in proximity, but they do bring it together in direction. These strategies may include creating a daily prayer guide, making an online prayer calendar, or having leaders agree to lead prayer toward a specific direction for a certain period of time. There is great advantage in that extra meetings do not have to be coordinated. The disadvantage is not being able to measure the true level of participation. Focused strategies depend heavily on the leaders of the ministries to adopt the strategy, communicate the vision, and build the strategy into the rhythms of their ministry.

One of the ways we attempted to focus our prayers at UT was to create a daily prayer guide for students to use in their personal devotional time. We had 31 campus ministers write a daily devotion with a scripture, a few thoughts about the scripture, and prayer points for UT from the scripture. We printed these prayer guides for every student so that we could be reading and praying the same things throughout a year. It was awesome to hear each pastor's heart for UT expressed through the scriptural prayers he or she submitted for the prayer guide, and it helped students see that we were all working together.

For a few years we had something we called the "Prayer Accord." Students who signed up for the Prayer Accord committed to three things: personally pray for UT daily, corporately pray for UT weekly, and fast for UT once a month on the first Friday of the month. Each week I would e-mail students a simple scripture and focus of prayer for the week that they could use to pray daily in their quiet times and weekly in their campus ministry prayer time. It united the campus in praying for one specific thing each week and served as a great way to direct prayers toward our campus-wide vision.

Saturation Prayer

Saturation prayer strategies are those that unite the body in praying for large segments of the campus, saturating the campus in prayer. Saturation strategies usually focus more on intercessory prayer, aimed at praying for specific people. Paul tells Timothy, "I urge, then, first of all, that requests, prayers, intercession, and thanksgiving be made for everyone — for kings and all those in authority" (I Timothy 2:1–2). These strategies are an attempt to do just that — to pray for everyone.

In 2003, UT had its largest freshman class in history, with over 8,000 new freshmen that fall semester. That fall we held an event where we printed all 8,000 names and had several days of 24-hour prayer to pray for each student by name. While intercessory prayer is certainly more effective where there is real relationship with the one for whom you are praying, this was a great way to intercede, if only for a few days, for literally 8,000 students.

Similarly, in obedience to the second part of Paul's command to pray for authorities, one year we launched an initiative called "Adopt-a-Prof." At the time, UT had about 2,100 professors, so we made 700 cards with three professors' names on each and distributed them to students who would commit to regularly pray for the three professors by name. It was a simple but profound way to be in prayer for our authorities. It solicited prayer for professors on a regular basis which was great, though not as good as a strategy based on personal relationships.

One of the more relational saturation strategies we developed was something we called the "High Five." One year, many of the ministries adopted a prayer strategy which encouraged their students to write down the names of five unbelieving students they knew personally, and then commit to pray for them

daily. That year we distributed almost 2,000 "High Five" cards, which meant that if students were being faithful to the vision, we were praying for more than 10,000 UT students each day. Because of the real relationships with these 10,000 students, prayers were more focused, and God used the students who were praying to be an answer to many of their own prayers.

Continuous Prayer

Continuous prayer strategies are those that unite the body in 24/7 prayer for the campus. Continuous prayer creates a great sense of momentum and oneness. The idea of handing off a prayer time to someone else who hands it off to another creates a sense of being in battle together. Continuous prayer is a practice of many traditions, from Catholic monasteries to the Moravian movement to campus houses of prayer today. There is something about continuous prayer that captures hearts and creates movement.

For two years, we had a 168-hour prayer chain at UT. I remember, as a student, spending my summers writing 15-week prayer guides to give to all 168 students that took an hour of prayer so that we could direct our prayer and make it easier for students to pray for one hour by themselves. Each year we would go to the campus ministries soliciting people to take one hour a week to pray for UT. For several semesters we were praying for the campus 24/7. It's not that difficult really, given that 168 people is not a lot and that students have no problem praying at 3 a.m. like most people would. For several years the UT prayer chain gave students a vision for giving God "no rest, until he establishes [the University of Texas] and makes her the praise of the earth" (Isaiah 62:7).

More recently, since 2006, the Campus House of Prayer (CHOP) has been the primary prayer mobilization strategy for us at UT. It seems that, in recent years, God has given many students a vision for 24/7 prayer. The International House of Prayer (IHOP) in Kansas City and its One Thing conferences, in addition to the 24/7 movement in England and Pete Grieg's book *Red Moon Rising,* have been used by God to generate a new movement of 24/7 prayer among college students. Campus Renewal Ministries, Campus America, Luke 18, and Campus Church Networks are all national campus ministries that are actively mobilizing prayer on college campuses. Since it appears that this is something God is doing on campuses, I thought it worth explaining in greater detail how we came to adopt the CHOP as a our primary prayer mobilization strategy.

When we began to sense God leading us to start the Campus House of Prayer, we first attempted periods of 24/7 prayer during Rez Week in order to give students a taste and hunger for it. For five years we did this, each year following up with students from the ministries who participated to ask them if they would be interested in seeing 24/7 prayer happen at UT beyond Rez Week. Each year, however, there was no traction with students. Similarly, in our Campus Minister Council meetings I would propose the idea, and each time the ministers would say, "It's not time yet."

Honestly, over the next few years, I found myself trying to make it happen until one day God told me, "Stop!" During Lent of 2006, I felt God very strongly tell me to stop planning and stop meeting with students and ministers to try to start the CHOP. Instead, God told me to prayerwalk the campus every day for 40 days and ask Him to establish the CHOP. I responded in obedience, and for 40 days I prayerwalked UT, asking for God to give us students committed to 24/7 prayer and a place to pray 24/7. I also made a vow of silence that Lent, committing not to talk to anyone about 24/7 prayer. For weeks I walked the campus and prayed for people and a place. The Lord had me focus my prayers on three possible buildings that could be home to the Campus House of Prayer, so I started to pray for them specifically.

My vow of silence was tested when I spoke to a group of students over spring break who had stayed in Austin to pray and do local service projects every day. One morning they invited me to speak to them. I had them watch one of the Sentinel Group's *Transformations* videos and then talk about what would need to happen to see revival at UT. Next, we prayed. The prayer time erupted into a time of prayer where everyone was praying aloud at the same time, asking God for a place for 24/7 prayer on campus. It was one of the most memorable prayer gatherings I have ever experienced. Afterward, the students started talking about how they could get a CHOP on campus. I listened and did not say a thing.

That semester, CRM had partnered with Campus America and Campus Church Network to get the whole semester covered in 24/7 prayer. We needed just 15 campuses each to commit to one week of 24-hour prayer in order to accomplish the goal of having a semester covered in prayer. We ended up with more than 70 campuses covering the semester in prayer! Most days three or more campuses across the United States were praying 24 hours a day. Clearly God was up to something, but I could not tell anyone.

Rez Week was during Lent that year, and we were again praying 24/7 that week as a part of the event. Every year we would put a clipboard in the Rez Week house of prayer that said, "I would like to make 24/7 prayer happen at UT." Usually 10 to 15 people would sign the clipboard, but when we followed up with each of them, very few actually thought they would be committed to an ongoing CHOP. That year, however, 75 students signed the clipboard! After Lent, when I was able to follow up with these 75 students, I found that almost all of them said they would love to be part of an ongoing CHOP, if we had one.

There was, of course, the rather important detail of having a space. We had tried to have a house of prayer once before, and discovered that it needed to be very close to campus for students to be able to come in and out throughout the day like they did every year during Rez Week. When we attempted to have a CHOP farther off campus one semester, nobody participated.

Remember, I had been prayerwalking the campus and had been asking for God to give us one of three open spaces. Shortly after Rez Week a campus pastor from one of the local churches called to ask if we would be interested in subleasing their building, as they were moving their offices and church. Aware of that possibility, theirs was one of the buildings I was praying for each day as I prayerwalked. When this building became available, we believed it was God's provision. God was clearly opening the doors and raising up a number of students with a vision for a place of 24/7 prayer and worship. The last step was to meet with the campus ministers, who unanimously agreed, "It is time."

After years of trying to make it happen, it took just 40 days of prayer and waiting to see God make it happen. It was certainly not due to my prayers and silence. That was just God's purpose for me. The fact is that it was God's timing. The Campus House of Prayer was the next step for us in prayer mobilization on our campus.

Now we have a beautiful building right off of UT's campus. It is close enough for students to walk to between classes to pray and right next to the highly populated west campus area where thousands of students live. Students sign up for an hour of prayer and commit to pray in the CHOP at that time every week. Most semesters we have 5 A.M. to midnight covered every day. We're still seeking God for a plan to get the morning hours covered on a daily basis. However, it's less about getting the hours filled and more about building a movement of students hungry for God to move in their lives and in the lives of their friends.

Many of the 63 campus ministries at UT have their weekly prayer time in the CHOP. Most hours, however, are filled by missional communities praying for the parts of UT where they are living on mission, such as dorms, fraternities, ethnic groups, sports teams, clubs, and majors. This what excites us the most — the CHOP is not just a random place of prayer, but a strategic place that builds unity and fuels the united mission.

" I still remember the first time I walked up to the CHOP as a freshman at the University of Texas at Austin. A student leader in my campus ministry had invited me to pray with her during her weekly prayer hour. I knocked on the door, shaking with nerves because the longest amount of time I had prayed consecutively was probably about 30 minutes. Stepping into that building was the best thing I could have done as a freshman in college, and it changed the course of my life. Up to that point, prayer had been obligatory and even painstaking for me. But as I stepped into the prayer room, I began to experience a living God. This God desired intimacy and free-flowing communication with me. In that first prayer meeting, and the hundreds more over the next four years, I and others met with our Father, who loved, disciplined, nourished, put fire in us, and gave us vision.

Not only did my relationship with God deepen, but I also became a part of a community that was passionate about seeking God for transformation on our campus. As I prayed with others at the CHOP, I began to form relationships with people that were founded in prayer and relationship with God. My first conversations with some of these friends was through prayer. To this day, those I met at the CHOP are my dearest friends.

This community took part in a retreat toward the end of my sophomore year of college called the "Revival Retreat." As we explored the history and principles of revival, God began to implant seeds in each of our hearts, "fireseeds of revival" to be exact. Our time spent praying and worshipping as a group drew the Holy Spirit until we could feel God's presence thick in the air. We were overcome with mourning for our campus and simultaneously a passion to see it transformed for the glory of God.

During this retreat God called me to be baptized. When I asked Him in prayer if it was the right time, He responded immediately with one of the retreat attendees hilariously falling in a nearby river. It was in this same river that I was baptized by Justin Christopher, whom I consider a spiritual father to me and so many others at the CHOP.

Out of this group was birthed a weekly prayer meeting called Revival Prayer. We gathered every Monday night that semester on the steps of the main campus building, the University of Texas

Tower, where students passed by continually. Our prayer and worship drew God's presence, and we were very aware that the spiritual atmosphere on our campus was changing. **"**

CELIA LUGO
Sigma Phi Lambda Christian Sorority
UT GRADUATE, 2010

Where to Start

Prayer is always the place to start. It is the place where God changes us, the place where the spiritual battle is won, and the place where vision is birthed so that the strategies are not man-made. You should begin by starting a Fusion Group. As the leaders grow in relationship and vision, God will lead you to some specific prayer mobilization event such as a concert of prayer, a prayerwalk, or something else. As you continue to grow in relationship and vision, you will be able to move forward in one of many different long-term prayer strategies. You can then use the prayer mobilization events to launch specific strategies. After several semesters, the Body of Christ will be working together in a significant way to mobilize the kind of prayer that typically precedes revival, perhaps even establishing a place of 24/7 prayer that is shared by all of the campus ministries. You will be pushing back the spiritual forces on your campus, making it possible to move forward with the campus-reaching vision.

spiritual
MAPPING

" THE SYSTEMATIC GATHERING AND EVALUATION OF DATA THROUGH SURVEYS, RESEARCH, AND SPIRITUAL PERCEPTIONS IN ORDER TO DISCOVER THE FACTORS, INFLUENCES, AND TRENDS THAT DETER OR ADVANCE GOD'S WORK ON CAMPUS. "

Campus Renewal Ministries is often invited by students or campus pastors to come to a campus to share how the Body of Christ can partner together in prayer and mission. One of the first things we do is ask the leaders to give their best guess at the number of students on their campus involved in a campus ministry, how many campus ministries are on campus, how many students put their faith in Christ in a given year, and how many missional communities they would need in order to reach every student community on campus. We have them write down their answers separately before we compare their best guesses. In some cases they have very similar answers. Most often, however, their answers are quite different from one another. Usually the larger ministries have a more positive perception of what God is doing on campus, whereas the smaller ministries' guesses are much lower. It makes sense that the groups having hundreds in attendance at worship each week would assume that other groups are experiencing the same thing. The same would be true for the ministries that are struggling. The truth about what God is doing on campus, however, can never really be discovered until the leaders from various ministries are in trusting relationships with one another — the type of relationships where they can share what God is doing in their ministries and be free from comparison, envy, and pride. An accurate account of the four simple questions we ask campus leaders cannot be measured until every ministry is at the table with a posture of humility and a vision to work as one Body to reach every student on campus.

The second year that our campus ministers met with Jim Herrington, we walked through the same discussion that led us to the goal of prayer mobilization the year before, but this time we felt God was directing us toward taking the next step of spiritual mapping. We had little to go on as reference points. Sure, every ministry did some sort of assessment of their work at the end of the year, and many ministries had some sort of year-end report that they were required by their churches and organizations to complete. For some, however, these organizational reports measured and valued things their local ministry did not care to measure because they did not fit the context of campus ministry at UT or were based on older campus ministry philosophies. The possibility of creating our own spiritual map was exciting because we could ask the questions that we thought were most important. We could define success and ask the questions we collectively thought could help measure that success.

That year we did two simple surveys. First, we created a year-end report for every campus ministry to complete, so we could get an accurate picture of the whole Body of Christ at UT. This survey let us know how many students were involved in campus ministry, how many students were in leadership within campus ministries, how many students had put their faith in Christ that year, the composition of ministries by ethnicity and classification, which unbelieving communities were being reached by campus ministries, and much more. Second, we created a survey for the Christian students within our ministries to help us understand where we needed to focus our discipleship efforts. This survey asked questions about where students lived, how often they shared their faith, how often they prayed and read the Bible, their spiritual background, their activities outside our campus ministries, how many campus ministries they were a part of, and more. We administered these surveys at the end of the spring semester, and over the summer I wrote an executive summary of the data, compiling it into a publication we called the *Longhorn Chronicles*.

THE TRUTH ABOUT WHAT GOD IS DOING ON CAMPUS, HOWEVER, CAN NEVER REALLY BE DISCOVERED UNTIL THE LEADERS FROM VARIOUS MINISTRIES ARE IN TRUSTING RELATIONSHIPS WITH ONE ANOTHER — THE TYPE OF RELATIONSHIPS WHERE THEY CAN SHARE WHAT GOD IS DOING IN THEIR MINISTRIES AND BE FREE FROM COMPARISON, ENVY, AND PRIDE.

The following October (after the September rush) we gathered for our first Campus Minister Luncheon where the results of the *Longhorn Chronicles* were revealed. During that meeting, we spent several hours in conversation about the findings. We have continued to host the Campus Minister Luncheon every year since, and it has become one of our liveliest gatherings. Every October, 70 to 90 campus ministers come together for five hours of conversation about what God is doing at UT. We discuss the *Longhorn Chronicles,* hear testimonies from many of the ministries, share a meal, and toss around ideas for the future. I liken it to a yearly State of the Union address, though it is really more of a conversation. Each year we develop UT's spiritual map further. As a result, campus ministries know where to partner, where their niche is, and where the need is, so that the entire campus can be reached with the gospel.

" One day each year every campus minister at the University of Texas blocks off a day to share a meal, celebrate God's work on campus, and to bear witness to God's saving work in our midst. If a new ministry forms, we all rejoice together. If several ministries are working together to bring an event to campus, we're all given the chance to participate. This luncheon is geared to remind us of the greatest biblical truth there is: "There is one body and one Spirit, one hope of your calling, one Lord, one faith, one baptism, one God and Father of all" (Ephesians 4:4–5). In other words, there is only one Lord, one Body, and our call is to work together.

We all leave the luncheon with a better sense of the big picture, like how many campus ministries exist and what areas are being reached or neglected. We are also all challenged. Two years ago, I had never heard of missional communities. Today I'm working and praying to foster them in my community. The relationships we build, the testimonies we hear, and the conversations that take place make the luncheon incredibly valuable.

This past year an African American campus minister, who is a former UT student, gave his testimony. Through tears he shared how a horrible experience of racism by a certain fraternity had brought him to Christ. I felt ashamed because I belonged to that fraternity when he had that experience. I knew Jesus wanted me to approach him, introduce myself, and apologize. It was a humbling and powerful moment of grace. We hugged, he accepted my apology, and I shared my testimony with him. It's hard to express what a powerful reminder that was that there's only one Lord and that our call is to work together.

JOHN NEWTON
Episcopal Student Center
CAMPUS MINISTER, 2008–PRESENT

The Biblical Basis for Spiritual Mapping

I am going to be honest. I don't believe that there are great scriptural mandates for spiritual mapping. Whereas I can make a solid biblical call for Fusion Groups, prayer mobilization, missional communities, and catalytic events, I believe there are no biblical commands to spiritually map the campus. There are, however, examples in the Bible where people practiced forms of spiritual mapping by examining the territory to which God was calling them. In addition to these scriptures, it seems obvious, as campus missionaries, that we should understand our campus.

Before Israel took the land (long before, as we sadly know), God told Moses, "Send some men to explore Canaan, which I am giving to the Israelites. From each ancestral tribe, send one of its leaders" (Numbers 13:2). God sent men out to explore the land. Before commissioning them Moses gave them seven different assignments, things they were to report on upon their return. Here God was sending men, united from every tribe, to scout out the land. Their report was meant to inspire faith and create a strategy for advancement. In this case, 10 of the 12 lacked faith, and God bound Israel to 40 years of wandering. Still, God sent them on a spiritual mapping campaign first. What we find in our initial spiritual mapping efforts may discourage us, but it should motivate us to pray, calling in faith on God's strength to accomplish transformation!

The night before he was going to challenge people to start rebuilding the wall, Nehemiah sneaked out in the middle of the night to spiritually map the land. The following day he was going to give a message to mobilize God's people for a specific mission. "I set out during the night with a few men. I had not told anyone what God had put in my heart to do for Jerusalem. There were no mounts with me except the one I was riding on. By night I went through the Valley Gate toward the Jackal Well and the Dung Gate, examining the walls of Jerusalem, which had been broken down, and its gates, which had been destroyed by fire. Then I moved toward the Fountain Gate and the King's Pool, but there was not enough room for my mount to get through; so I went up the valley by night, examining the wall" (Nehemiah 2:12–15). Before Nehemiah called those released from exile to join him in rebuilding the wall, he first examined the wall for himself. Nehemiah had a very detailed plan for rebuilding the wall. In fact, though there was opposition, they rebuilt the wall in just 52 days! He would never have had the clarity of vision had he not taken his prayerwalk (prayer-ride, for him) to see the extent of the destruction and what was needed to bring restoration.

We will better know how to lead our ministries when we have an accurate picture of the exact problems we are facing. Good leaders seek this information and take it to God in prayer so that they can receive His plan for transformation. We need to know the true state of our campuses in order to have a plan for transformation. Uniting in order to spiritually map the campus allows us to see more than our small pictures. It allows us to see the whole, and thus we can teach, disciple, pray, plan, and act in a way to bring transformation.

Paul practiced a form of spiritual mapping too. "While Paul was waiting for them in Athens, he was greatly distressed to see the city was full of idols" (Acts 17:16). While waiting for Timothy and Silas, Paul surveyed Athens. He found them to be a very religious people, pluralistic, with many gods. Knowing the heart condition of the Athenians, his thoughts and prayers led him to a specific message related to their altar "To an Unknown God." After spiritually mapping the land, he tailored a message revealing Jesus as their "unknown god." After his message "many sneered, but others said, 'We want to hear you again on this subject'" (Acts 17:32).

A few even put their faith in Jesus immediately after the message. Paul, as a missionary, studied his people group, and was therefore able to explain the gospel in a way that created a hunger in many to hear more. As missionaries to our campuses, why would we not want to know more about our mission field? As campus missionaries, we need to know the state of the campus,

AS CAMPUS MISSIONARIES, WE NEED TO KNOW THE STATE OF THE CAMPUS, WHO IS DOING WHAT WHERE, WHAT OUR STUDENTS ARE STRUGGLING WITH, WHAT COMMUNITIES REMAIN UNREACHED, WHAT IS WORKING FOR OTHER MINISTRIES, WHAT TOOLS WE COULD SHARE, AND WHERE WE CAN PARTNER.

who is doing what where, what our students are struggling with, what communities remain unreached, what is working for other ministries, what tools we could share, and where we can partner. I often hear about how overseas missionaries are partnering to reach people groups because of the sheer need they have for laborers. Somehow on our campuses, because we're focusing on the Christians instead of the lost students, we don't sense the same dire need to partner together, to treat the whole campus as a mission field. If we did, we'd surely share information and collaborate to spiritually map the campus.

Don't Underestimate the Process

Often when we tell leaders from other campuses what information we have gathered at UT through spiritual mapping, they say,

"Can you send us the surveys you have used to gather this information?" We almost always answer, "No." The process of bringing leaders together to determine what information you want to know and why is invaluable. These conversations help leaders understand what each ministry values, and the lens through which they view the transformation of their campus. It also helps define the goal of your partnership, setting parameters through which you can tell if your partnership is impacting the campus.

I remember sitting in a room with campus ministers when we wrote on a dry erase board everything we wanted to know about the campus, our students, and our campus ministries. The conversation itself helped us focus on ways we thought we could measure transformation. It clarified our vision tremendously. A few weeks later we met to write a survey that we could distribute to every campus ministry to complete. Now every February we meet to make small changes to the survey. We change questions, add questions, and subtract questions depending on what we want to know. That said, we try to ask many of the same questions each year, so that we can compare one year to the next. The process is important, no matter what kind of spiritual mapping you attempt. It is important that you bring leaders together to discuss what you want to know and why, and to work together to create tools to gather that information.

I should warn you, however, that while creating the surveys can be a life-giving process, collecting the surveys is a frustratingly difficult process. Every year at the end of April, we distribute our online surveys to every campus ministry director (63 surveys in 2010). We give the leaders one month to complete the survey. It seems reasonable to expect them to be able to block out 10 to 15 minutes sometime in May to complete the survey, but there are always a few that need a little extra encouragement. It's the only thing we do all year that we require 100 percent participation. Otherwise, the data would be inaccurate. The leaders who are most connected and who have been a part of the process of creating the survey each year complete the survey willingly. Those that are less connected and unfamiliar with the process and purposes of the survey are naturally less motivated to participate. Getting everyone to complete a year-end survey takes a lot of communication and grace — something we have done well at times and sometimes not so well.

Types of Spiritual Mapping

Year-end Surveys

One of the most important ways to spiritual map your campus is to create year-end surveys for every campus ministry to complete. It allows you to get an accurate picture of the Body of Christ on your campus. You can see how many students are involved in campus ministry, how many are in discipleship, how many put their faith in Christ, the number of campus ministers and volunteers reaching out to the campus, the ethnic diversity of the Body of Christ, and more. Conducting a survey like this every year shows you where God is moving. From our year-end surveys, for instance, we've learned that the Latino students are the least

Longhorn Chronicles	2002	2006	2010
New believers	297	357	625
Students involved in campus ministries	2680	3991	4962
Missional communities	0	88	218
Campus ministries	40	52	63
Campus ministers	87	137	175
Students in leadership	660	815	1060
Students on spring break and summer missions	750	996*	984

*higher than normal due to Hurricane Katrina relief

involved in campus ministry, that we're reaching a lot of international students from north Asia, but very few from other parts of the world, and that 14 new campus ministries and churches have been birthed over the last four years. Year-end surveys give you an accurate picture of the Body of Christ on your campus. Plus, creating a list of campus ministries and their contact information in order to distribute the survey is a spiritual mapping exercise in and of itself!

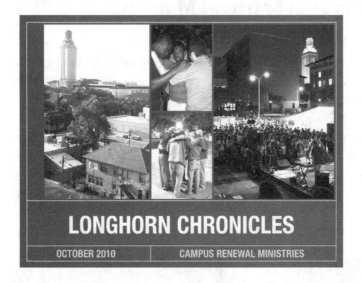

LONGHORN CHRONICLES

OCTOBER 2010 | CAMPUS RENEWAL MINISTRIES

You can view the latest edition of the *Longhorn Chronicles* each year on Campus Renewal Ministries' UT website: www. texasunited.org.

Christian Surveys

We try to conduct surveys for the Christian community every four years. Just like we do with the year-end survey, we bring out the previous survey and fine-tune it, adding a few questions and removing a few. The difficult part is trying to keep the survey under 50 questions. We actually conduct it on Scantron sheets so that students can answer anonymously. We're able to process our Scantrons through UT's testing center. It takes just minutes to get the results. Creating surveys for students within your ministries is a helpful way to understand the strengths, weaknesses, issues, struggles, and strongholds in the Christian community. You can use what you learn from these studies to shape your discipleship process, what you teach, and what catalytic events you need to plan.

In 2001, we discovered that 69 percent of our students were involved in two or more ministries and that only 40 percent were involved in an unbelieving community on campus, such as a club, sports team, or scholastic organization. Believing this was a problem, we agreed to continually remind students to be involved in just one campus ministry and to adopt a mission field by getting involved in one other community on campus. Three years later, we found that 56 percent of students were connecting in some unbelieving community on campus. These statistics show how valuable surveys of the Christian community can be. Even if we may intrinsically know the problems students are facing, firm statistical data can confirm your assumptions and shape the way you speak into students' lives.

In 2008, we learned from our Christian student survey that 34 percent of Christian men look at pornography once a week or more and 72 percent of Christian women feel bad about the way they look once a week or more. We knew this was a huge problem, but having the data right in front of us set us on a track to host a united event called the "Power of Porn" where a male and female speaker shared about the damaging effects of pornography on their lives. We used what we learned to shape a catalytic event.

Below you can read some of what we learned from our most recent Christian student survey conducted in 2008. You will see some encouraging signs along with some that are very discouraging. You can see how Christian student surveys can help leaders in the Body of Christ know where to focus their discipleship.

Evangelism

- 56% "hang out" with someone from another country once a week or more
- 26% have spiritual conversations with unbelieving friends once a week or more
- 32% have spiritual conversations with unbelieving friends once a semester or less

Ministry Involvement

- 69% are involved in two or more campus ministries
- 20% are involved in three or more campus ministries

Theology

- 8% believe other religious books are equally inspired as the Bible
- 12% believe parts of the Bible are not historical or true

Family

- 63% say their parents have an "excellent" or "healthy" marriage
- 57% put their faith in Christ before middle school

Devotional Life

- 72% read the Bible three times a week or more
- 68% spend time in prayer daily

Struggles and Behaviors

- 26% get drunk once a semester or more
- 13% of women struggle with an eating disorder
- 34% of men look at pornography once a week or more
- 20% feel depressed once a week or more
- 24% have had intercourse or oral sex within the last year
- 70% have never had intercourse or oral sex

Recreation

- 63% play sports or exercise one to two hours a day
- 53% spend three or more hours a day on the computer (*not including school work*)

On-Campus Surveys

Partnering to interview hundreds of students on campus can lead to a greater understanding of students' worldviews, social concerns, fears, needs, spiritual backgrounds, perceptions of Christians, and understanding of the gospel. In addition, the process itself is eye-opening to students involved with campus ministry and can create opportunities for further spiritual discussion. In 2004, we organized 80 students from eight different ministries to conduct 800 interviews on campus. We intentionally chose 80 locations that different types of students frequent. At each location we conducted 10 interviews. I personally remember interviewing students at JP's Java, where math and science students hang out, in addition to many grad students; Posse East Pub, where music students, fraternity guys, and the student happy hour crowd hang out; and the Malcolm X lounge, where African American students hang out. Students from these three communities alone had extremely different responses to my interviews.

We conducted all 800 interviews in one week and brought the 80 students together to debrief. The conversation was electric. Students began to realize that because UT was made up of many people groups, the gospel had to be introduced to each one in different ways. The experience alone was worth the time and effort, but the data compiled was even more valuable. The information from the interviews was imported to an Excel file and given to each ministry so that everyone could see the responses from various students and locations — Jester Dormitory, African Americans, West Campus, international students, the business school, the engineering school, Greek organizations, etc. At our Campus Minister Council in the spring of 2010, we met to plan our next set of on-campus surveys. It has been six years since we did anything like this, but we agreed to move forward on something similar next school year. We hope to conduct 1,000 surveys during the spring 2011 semester.

Often valuable data about students can be collected from university resources. Counseling centers frequently have statistics about mental illness and addictions. Psychology and sociology classes have students do surveys on campus, and the results may be published or can be gathered with permission. These can be good free resources for revealing the health and activities of students. To understand the spiritual condition of students, however, you would need to partner to create your own surveys.

Historical Studies

Part of spiritual mapping includes further in-depth study of the history of your campus in order to confess and repent for sins of the past, address inherited strongholds, or pray along the lines of past revivals and the original purposes of your university (many of which have Christian foundations). Perhaps your campus has a sad history of racism. Perhaps there was a time when your university expressly broke with its Christian heritage. Perhaps your campus has a history of rioting. Perhaps your campus has had a number of professors who have led the way in removing God from their disciplines of study. Perhaps your campus has experienced great periods of revival. Knowing where you have come from can help direct your prayer and plans for the future. At UT, we found one thing in particular which we needed to confess and pray for repentance.

In 1941, a group of UT students consulted a fortuneteller regarding an 18-year losing streak against the Texas A&M Aggies at Kyle Field. The fortuneteller, Madame Augusta Hipple, who practiced fortunetelling through occult practices, instructed the students to burn red candles in their homes and stores a week prior to the next game at Kyle Field to break the jinx A&M had placed on the Longhorns. Through the week of Thanksgiving, candles were burned in store windows along the Drag, in the fraternity and sorority houses of West Campus, in the lounges of university residence halls, and in the windows of houses in

Austin's neighborhoods. That year A&M lost to UT in a 23–0 defeat, and UT finished fourth in the national AP poll. This ritual soon became known as the Hex Rally, and over the years UT used bonfires, torches, and now, since 1986, practices the hex by lighting candles at a pep rally in the middle of campus. Several years ago, we invited leaders from the Body of Christ at Texas A&M to come to UT during the Hex Rally. There we asked for their forgiveness for cursing them, prayed blessings over them, and prayed for God to bring an end to this tradition. For now, the tradition still exists, though we continue to make it a day of prayer for Texas A&M University.

Texans have a bad reputation for thinking we're better than other states. As the saying goes, "Everything is bigger in Texas." I'll never forget when I brought Brent Kanyok, CRM staff at Florida State, to a UT football game. The band was playing several Texas songs before the game began, and a student yelled at the top of his lungs, "Texas is superior to all other states!" Brent got a good laugh, as it confirmed his preconceived (and true) notions that we are a prideful state. For years UT's official slogan was simply "We're Texas." Every radio or television commercial for UT ended with that phrase. Knowing that God resists the proud, but gives grace to the humble, many of us started praying for humility and repenting of pride (both in the Body of Christ and on campus overall). Since that time, we've seen an incredible amount of humility in the Body of Christ, and UT even changed its official slogan to "What starts here changes the world." Now that's a slogan we can agree with.

People Group Studies

I will share more about this in the chapter on missional communities, but one of the aims of your spiritual map is to identify people groups on campus — which ones are being reached with the gospel and which are not, where you have students living on mission and where you do not. You need to understand where distinct communities of students exist, such as sports teams, dorms, political organizations, spirit groups, co-operative living houses, ethnic groups, international students, bohemians, IM sports, service organizations, Greek organizations, etc. If you are partnering together to see the campus as one large mission field, then you need to identify specific communities you want to reach with the gospel. You need to know which campus ministries are reaching specific people groups so that you can identify where to partner together (where you share common influence) and where to focus attention on new communities (where no one is reaching).

The last questions we ask on our year-end survey are about where each ministry intentionally has students on mission. We compile all of this information into the *Longhorn Chronicles* so that ministries can identify who they can partner with to reach specific communities. For instance, Hyde Park Baptist Church and Texas Wesley United Methodist Campus Ministry each have students who have committed to live on mission in San Jacinto Dormitory. Their students have partnered together to live and share the gospel in that dorm. The same is true of Hill Country Bible Church UT, The Austin Stone Community Church, and Campus Renewal Ministries, who have nursing students on mission in their department. We have had a great group of students on mission in the Civil and Architectural Engineering department, but not in the other engineering departments. Aware of this, we have called students from many different ministries to partner on mission in Aerospace, Chemical, and Mechanical Engineering school this next fall. A significant part of our spiritual map is keeping track of which people groups at UT are being reached and which are not. We are not just measuring number growth as a means of success. We're measuring how far we have gone each year in reaching the whole campus with the gospel, because some day we hope to see a missional community in every college, club, residence, and culture at UT!

" Through the years we've made a number of different attempts at understanding both our ministries and our campus to the best of our ability, from listing out every club, residence, college/major, and other affinities we could identify, to surveying students on their spiritual attitudes and worldviews, and even identifying strongholds the enemy has had on the campus for several decades. Although we are far from having a detailed understanding of every corner of our campus, we have realized that through hard work, asking some specific questions, and using information that is already available, we can have a very functional understanding of the sociological and spiritual map of our campus.

There are two key components to mapping: understanding ministries and the ways they are actually engaging the campus, and understanding the "people groups" that exist on campus. One of the chief benefits of having a comprehensive understanding of the people groups on your campus is knowing where you are effective, and where opportunities exist for students and ministries to engage next.

Through surveying the fruit of different ministries over the years with the *Longhorn Chronicles*, coupled with a broad understanding of student groups, we've seen that there are certain groups of people that are easier to engage because the students in them have a high degree of relational overlap for a longer period of time.

Fraternities and sororities present an excellent example of these kinds of people groups because they serve as the primary community for the students that belong to them. At UT, fraternities and sororities are some of a few places that we have seen long-term, sustainable fruit on campus and generational change. Dorms have been places that are often difficult to create a sustaining ministry because of the high degree of student turnover from year to year. This doesn't mean that it isn't valuable to do dorm ministry; it just makes it that much more difficult for a gospel presence to be sustained by indigenous missionary students year after year.

Finally, in understanding your own ministry, those around you, and the campus you are trying to reach, you become aware of places where efforts are being duplicated. Early on in the process, when we began seeking to understand where each ministry was already engaged, six campus ministers were sitting around a table talking about what God was doing. Shortly, we realized that three of us had students ministering independently of one another in the same dorm, and no one knew what the others were doing. Rather than all three ministries trying to support three independent efforts, we connected the students to one another, and one ministry took over the role of coaching those particular students, freeing up precious time for investment in other areas of campus. This story has been repeated numerous times across ministry lines to connect students together with a common heart and shared relational networks. 〞

TODD ENGSTROM
The Austin Stone Community Church
CAMPUS MINISTER, 2005–PRESENT

Informing Prayer and Mission

Spiritual mapping is meant to inform prayer and mission. When we know more about what sinful strongholds and worldviews are affecting the spiritual climate of our campuses, then we know how to pray. We can corporately confess sin on behalf of the Body of Christ and our campus at large. We can ask God to reveal sin and give us repentant hearts. We can ask Him to free us from our past and reveal to us a new future. We can pray specifically, because we have real data to inform our prayers.

Additionally, we can act intentionally. When we know the problems we are facing, we can seek God for a specific plan of action. We can collaborate on catalytic events aimed at addressing a particular issue. We can unite to teach the same things to our students with one prophetic voice. We can partner in mission to reach specific unreached people groups on campus, and we can know how to uniquely contextualize the gospel to each of these people groups.

missional communities
(SPARK groups)

" GROUPS OF CHRIST FOLLOWERS UNITED IN PRAYER AND MISSION TO DEMONSTRATE AND DECLARE THE GOSPEL OF JESUS AND MAKE DISCIPLES FROM WITHIN A SPECIFIC PEOPLE GROUP. "

After a few years of praying together and working to develop our spiritual map, we had a pretty complete picture of the Body of Christ at UT. Assumptions we had were made more concrete by our data, and in many cases, new truths were revealed that we would have never known otherwise. Several things we discovered were important factors leading to our next step in the campus-reaching process.

We realized that only 300 students a year were beginning to follow Jesus for the first time. Many ministries did not see one student put their faith in Jesus during the course of the school year. Most saw only one or two students do so. We also realized that our ministries were filled with students who had come from Christian homes. Fifty-seven percent of students in our ministries put their faith in Jesus as a child, and another 32 percent did so in junior high or high school. Eighty-nine percent of our students were walking with God before they came to UT, while only 10 percent began their walk with the Lord while on campus. The fact was that we were not reaching unbelieving students with the gospel of Jesus. For the most part, we were just building a community for the Christian students that came to UT. Add to this the fact that 60 percent of our students did not have any unbelieving friends and only 26 percent had spiritual conversations with their unbelieving friends more than once a month. No wonder that no more than 300 students would become believers each year.

City Reaching talks about the need to become a "go-to" church instead of a "come-to" church. After reading the book, we talked a lot about the need to go to the lost. We knew that if we wanted to see UT as one large mission field, we would need to partner together to send students as missionaries into the dorms, Greek houses, sports teams, academic departments, spirit groups, political organizations, ethnic student associations, social clubs, etc. Becoming a "go-to" church, however, was more difficult than we expected. The fact was that our staffing, money, time, resources, and training were all allocated to "come-to" methods of ministry.

I distinctly remember one of our gatherings with Jim Herrington when he drew a pyramid on the board and divided it into three parts. The largest part was labeled "thinking," the

middle "structures," and the smallest top "programs." He said,
"You guys have made the first shift in your thinking. You believe you need to be a go-to church. However, you have not
changed your structures to reflect your thinking. You can't just
try to change some programs. Your structures need to change."
Several ministries began to make that change. The Texas Wesley
United Methodist Campus Ministry, for instance, developed a
new leadership team called their "Outreach Council." Their Outreach Council did not plan outreach events. Rather, it consisted
of students who committed to reach out to a specific part of the
campus and met together weekly to tell stories and pray for their
various missions. One by one ministries started calling many
of their students out of certain ministry positions and into UT's
mission field. Staff and financial decisions were made to support
student missionaries, and we formed a partnership with Glenn
Smith, from New Church Initiatives, to begin training our student missionaries.

As our structures changed, we grew from having 20 missional communities in 2004 to 40 in 2005, 80 in 2006, 160 in 2007,
to 220 missional communities today. Last year, 625 UT students
began to follow Jesus. As our missional communities increased
so did the number of students being saved. The students themselves have experienced a change in their thinking. They have
begun to see themselves as God's missionaries to particular parts
of the campus, as indeed they are.

" Before coming to UT, I had never really merged the ideas
of prayer, service, and evangelism, much less imagined that I
could do all three among and in partnership with the people I'm
around every day. I first learned about missional communities
in the spring of my freshman year. I received coaching from an
older student to learn the biblical principles of reaching out to
my peers and began praying with another student for the Aerospace Engineering department.

During my second year at UT, my roommate Jared, who I knew through my campus ministry, was an RA (Resident Assistant) in San Jacinto Dorm. We held a Bible study in the dorm every week, mostly made up of guys from our ministry that we were pouring into and challenging to live on mission to reach their friends. At the same time, a couple of guys from other campus ministries had also committed to lead missional communities in our dorm, and we met with them frequently to pray together and encourage each other.

Because of Jared's position as an RA, we had a unique chance to witness to the other RAs in our dorm and even saw one RA move from totally rejecting the gospel at the beginning of the year to accepting Christ as his Savior in April! At the same time, the Christian guys in our Bible study have grown more comfortable in their faith and are beginning to understand that our purpose as believers is to share God's love with others.

In the fall of 2010 (my third year at UT), we are building a network of missional communities in the Cockrell School of Engineering. In each engineering department (Aerospace, Chemical, Civil, Mechanical, etc.), we are bringing together a group of believers from a variety of different campus ministries. Each group meets weekly to pray and encourage one another to be intentional in reaching out to their peers. We are also creating a mentoring program to connect underclassmen with older students for academic, spiritual, and lifestyle guidance. "

PETER SCHULTE
Hyde Park Baptist Church
UT STUDENT, CLASS OF 2012

The Biblical Basis for Missional Communities

Incarnational Mission

In Jesus's longest recorded prayer in John 17, He said to His Father, "As you sent me into the world, I have sent them into the world" (John 17:18). Jesus is sending us the same way that

He was sent. So how was Jesus sent? He was sent incarnation-
ally. He left the holiest of huddles to dwell with sinful men — to
live, work, and play among them. Jesus is sending us to do the
same. He is calling us to get out of our holy huddles and build
relationships with communities of lost people.

Most Christian students are engaged in too many Christian activities. They are in Bible studies, on worship teams, and
on leadership teams. They attend worship services two or three
times a week and are often involved in more than one ministry. These activities, in addition to
studies and perhaps having a job,
crowd out time for relationships
outside of the Christian community. This cannot be what Jesus in-
tended for His people, when one of
His last prayers and His very last
words were about making disciples from within lost communities.

In the same prayer, Jesus says,
"My prayer is not that you take
them out of the world, but that
you protect them from the evil one.
They are not of the world, even as

**JESUS DID NOT WANT
HIS DISCIPLES TO
SEPARATE FROM THE
WORLD, BUT TO BE
SANCTIFIED BY TRUTH
IN THE MIDST OF THE
WORLD. HE WANTS TO
TRANSFORM OUR LIVES
SO THAT WE ARE IN THE
WORLD, BUT NOT OF
THE WORLD.**

I am not of it. Sanctify them by your truth, your word is truth"
(John 17:15–17). Jesus did not want His disciples to separate
from the world, but to be sanctified by truth in the midst of the
world. He wants to transform our lives so that we are in the
world, but not of the world.

Yet, so often believers have felt they needed to separate
from the world in order to be sanctified. Well-meaning parents
and youth pastors scare incoming freshmen into thinking they
will get sucked in by the temptations on college campuses. They
warn them to find a fellowship so that they do not lose their

faith. Of course, they should find fellowship, but they should not, out of fear of the world, separate themselves from other communities on campus by isolating themselves in Christian communities. They need to find fellowships that will disciple them and equip them to be missionaries in their classes, clubs, and residences.

My friend and fellow CRM staffer Raul Garcia tells the story of how he decided to add up all the hours he was spending in the campus ministries that he was a part of his junior year at UT. He was leading a small group, discipling some guys, heading up a missions trip, attending his church's college worship service during the week and their worship service on Sunday, in addition to coming to CRM's daily prayer and being on CRM's Rez Week leadership team. He calculated that he spent 20 or more hours a week doing "ministry stuff."

When he combined these commitments with his workload as a student, he realized he had no time for relationships with unbelievers. His busyness with ministry had also squeezed out what he loved to do recreationally: Run. As we began to call students to live on mission, he grew increasingly uncomfortable with these facts. He knew God was calling him to make time to build relationships within a specific community of unbelievers at UT.

That year, First Evangelical Free Church was launching its first missional communities. One was to the UT track team. Raul instantly connected with the leader of the group, and they partnered together to live and share the gospel with these elite athletes. Raul describes this as the year that changed his life. Getting out of the Christian bubble and into the lives of lost athletes showed Raul a whole new dimension of God's love and the depth of the gospel. He was not the only one changed, however. Several of the guys on the team began to follow Christ too. After graduating, Raul continues to reach out to athletes, as he is now a member of an elite running group in Austin, Texas.

In his book Sparks, *you can read a more personal account of Raul's story and the stories of others at UT who have learned how to get out of the Christian bubble and into the lives of those Jesus came to seek and save. The book can be purchased and/or downloaded at our website:* www.campusrenewal.org.

College is the time (if not earlier) to learn to be in the world, but not of it, as Jesus prayed. Imagine if hundreds of thousands of Christian students isolated themselves in Christian communities in college and never learned to integrate their faith into their disciplines of study and among their peers. You would end up with Christian adults in the marketplace and in neighborhoods who also isolate themselves, and our cities and nations would be without Christ. The Christian community ends up looking more like a club for members only. Some would argue, that this is already happening in our country and around the world. What we need is thousands of Christ followers graduating every year, having learned to walk with Jesus and live on mission among their peers. The student who knows how to live on mission in the engineering school will

> **COLLEGE IS THE TIME (IF NOT EARLIER) TO LEARN TO BE IN THE WORLD, BUT NOT OF IT, AS JESUS PRAYED.**

live like a missionary in the marketplace after school. This is the hope for our cities and the nations — an answer to Jesus's prayer.

Campus Saturation

Jesus's prayer the night before His death on the cross is similar to the words He spoke just before His ascension into heaven, when He said, "But you will receive power when the Holy Spirit comes on you; and you will be my witnesses in Jerusalem, and in all Judea and Samaria, and to the ends of the earth" (Acts 1:8). Jesus's prayer and His final words reveal what is on His heart. He wants to empower us to be witnesses to the gospel in our communities and the communities around us. It begins where we are (in the disciples' case, Jerusalem) and multiplies outward to other communities who have not heard the gospel (the ends of the earth).

WE ARE COLLECTIVELY SEEKING TO REDUCE THE LOSTNESS OF OUR CAMPUS. WE WANT TO SEE A MISSIONAL COMMUNITY IN EVERY COLLEGE, CLUB, RESIDENCE, AND CULTURE AT UT.

Jesus modeled this Himself. When some people were trying to keep Him from leaving their town, He said, "I must preach the good news of the kingdom of God to other towns also, because that is why I was sent" (Luke 4:43). Similarly, Paul said, "So from Jerusalem all the way around to Illyricum, I have fully proclaimed the gospel. It has always been my ambition to preach the gospel where Christ was not known" (Romans 15:19b–20a). Paul understood Jesus's promise to empower His people to take the gospel to the ends of the earth, and he lived his life as a fulfillment of this promise, literally saturating regions of the world with the gospel before moving on to regions that remained unreached.

Our campuses are little mission fields. At UT we have about 50,000 students, 21 varsity sports, dozens of competitive club sports, more than 1,000 student organizations, 15 departments, more than 100 majors, 10 dorms (one with more than 4,000 students), more than 40 fraternities and sororities, more than 30 ethnic student organizations, and 4,500 international students from dozens of different countries. We estimate that we have 500 distinct people groups that we hope to reach with the gospel of Jesus. Like Jesus and like Paul, we're aiming to send students to the communities that remain unreached. We are collectively seeking to reduce the lostness of our campus. We want to see a missional community in every college, club, residence, and culture at UT.

IMAGINE IF EVERY STUDENT ON CAMPUS HAD A FEW CHRISTIAN FRIENDS WHO WERE FAITHFUL TO DEMONSTRATE AND DECLARE THE GOSPEL TO HIM OR HER THROUGHOUT THE COURSE OF A SCHOOL YEAR OR LONGER. IF THIS WERE TRUE AND THE HOLY SPIRIT BROUGHT REVIVAL, YOU COULD LITERALLY DISCIPLE THE ENTIRE CAMPUS.

I make it a habit when I meet new students to ask where they live, what they are studying, what clubs they are a part of, and what they like to do for fun. I ask these questions so that I can determine where God might be calling them to live on mission. After I hear their responses to my questions, I can connect them with others already leading missional communities, or I can challenge them to start their own.

I met Rachel Alvarez her freshman year at UT when she came to the Campus House of Prayer. I asked her some of my normal questions and discovered she lived in a dorm where we did not have a missional community. We provided training, helped her connect with a few others, and she was off and running. She and her partners were faithful witnesses on their floor and were able to share the gospel with many students. When she moved out of the dorm, she had to reconsider where her missional community would be.

She met Natalie, a "person of peace" (Luke 10:6) at her apartment complex. Rachel and Natalie quickly started having spiritual conversations and began studying the Bible together. After a few weeks she put her faith in Christ. Natalie's roommates noticed the changes in her life and they became spiritually hungry as well. Soon Rachel and Natalie were studying the scriptures with six of Natalie's friends, and a few weeks later all six put their faith in Christ. Natalie's mom has also recently begun to follow Jesus. Next year Rachel is going to be a coach for several new missional community leaders at UT.

Imagine if every student on campus had a few Christian friends who were faithful to demonstrate and declare the gospel to him or her throughout the course of a school year or longer. If this were true and the Holy Spirit brought revival, you could literally disciple the entire campus. Students could be discipled by the mature believers they already spend time with almost every day, since they belong to the same teams, classes, dorms, clubs, etc. The campus is one mission field with hundreds of distinct communities. The key to seeing a campus reached with the gospel is equipping and planting missional communities within each of these distinct people groups so that every student can hear the gospel from a community of believers whom he or she knows and trusts.

How to Lead a Missional Community Movement

Making Time for Mission

In order to saturate a campus, you need students to lead missional communities. In order to send students out as missionaries, you need to require less from them within your ministries. Students cannot build meaningful relationships with students in their communities if they do not have time to do so. Often it is the campus ministries themselves that are the cause of Christian isolation. Students are stuck in their holy huddles because we have demanded it with all of our ministry activities and the sheer manpower needed to pull them off. We need to ask less of our students within our ministries and more of our students outside our ministries, but to do this we, too, need to be doing less. "Less is more" applies to our students and our ministries. One of the best ways we can disciple students, who are already a part of a generation distracted by technology and entertainment, is to help them focus on the few things God is calling them to do.

At UT, we dream of a day where every student is involved in one ministry and has one mission. Together, we started casting this vision, encouraging students to stop committing to two or three different ministries, or even to two or three teams within an individual ministry. When ministry leaders are praying together every week and in real trusting relationships with one another, it is much easier to challenge students who are involved in more than one ministry to pick just one. No one is territorial about which ministry students choose, but leaders are persistent in calling them to choose. There is no way that we can saturate the campus if students are too busy to make time for the lost. What if every believer on campus had just one Christian community that provided a great worship experience (teaching and music to engage the mind and heart) and great community in small groups (a place to be known and grow in relationships)? What if every believer on campus also had just one mission field, where she would partner with a few other believers to build relationships within a specific community and live and share the gospel with that community throughout the year? Wouldn't the gospel advance much further if students had such a simple commitment to one ministry and one mission?

> ONE OF THE BEST WAYS WE CAN DISCIPLE STUDENTS, WHO ARE ALREADY A PART OF A GENERATION DISTRACTED BY TECHNOLOGY AND ENTERTAINMENT, IS TO HELP THEM FOCUS ON THE FEW THINGS GOD IS CALLING THEM TO DO.

When it comes to mission, the starting point is to ask students where they already spend their time. Whenever I meet new students that are believers, I start asking questions about what ministry they are a part of and how they are connected within that ministry. I ask what they are studying, what they do for fun, who they spend time with, where they live, and where they hang out — all in an attempt to discern where they spend their time already. Then I challenge them to think about how they can spend time in those communities with greater gospel intentionality. I am not going to overwhelm them by suggesting they add something to their schedule. Instead, more often I suggest that they stop doing one or more things with their Christian friends so they can spend some time building meaningful relationships with the people that God has already placed around them. If a student has no connection with any unbelieving community, I ask him or her to identify things they already like to do and suggest they start doing the same things with unbelievers. If they like to dance, I don't want them to start the UT Christian Dance Club! Instead, I encourage them to join the Roustabout troop or to take a ballroom dance class.

" When I first planted Hill Country UT I had a very traditional model of ministry in mind. The first two years of the church were very successful in most people's minds. We grew exponentially and had a number of very good ministry tactics that seemed to be growing the church. However, after two years of ministry I began to evaluate our success. I came to realize that though we did a decent job at attracting students for the first two years, we only witnessed two students give their life to Jesus Christ. This is not why I started this church. My desire was to see students convert to Jesus Christ, not just attract a bunch of Christian kids.

This realization sent me back to the drawing board. I began to think in a new way: If I had no money, no building, no resources but a dozen students, what would I do differently? This transitioned my thinking to not just being a pastor, but a missiologist of our community. We spent the summer of 2007 reenvisioning our strategy to embrace a missional community model. I began to ask specific questions: How are we going to do ministry? How will we quickly equip our students to get on mission as fast as possible? What will be the measurement of success? And how will we manage our resources properly?

We settled on a simple philosophy of doing missional communities we call our "E3." We encourage our missional community leaders to: Engage a people group, Express their faith through spiritual conversations and acts of service, and Explore the truth of Jesus Christ through study of scripture with nonbelievers. We focused and trained all of our adults to become coaches and mentors who poured their lives into our students that we now consider missionaries. We coached and equipped our students in the areas of the E3 philosophy.

Along with the equipping and training we ensured that we reallocated both our human and financial resources to maximize our missional effort. We scrutinized our efforts with measurements. We began to measure what we thought was most important. For example: How many people did we engage this week relationally? How many spiritual conversations did our students have this week? How many gospel presentations did our missional communities have this week? How many future missional community leaders do we have in waiting?

Over the last three years not only has the missional community strategy become our model of how we reach the nonbelieving student at UT, but our Kingdom impact has grown exponentially. The first two years of the church we saw two new believers; the last three years we have seen hundreds come to know Jesus Christ.

The challenge for pastors considering a transition to a missional movement is that they must go through the agonizing process of reengineering their mindsets of how to do ministry. They must ask the questions: what will be the measures of success, how can we equip students quickly, and how can we leverage the resources of adults to coach and mentor? **"**

DENNY HENDERSON
Hill Country Bible Church UT
CAMPUS MINISTER, 2005–PRESENT

Coaching and Equipping

One of the most difficult aspects of developing a missional community movement is learning to equip students. The fact is that most campus ministries have never attempted to train students to be missional in a specific community. Many have curriculum designed to train their students how to share their testimony or how to share the gospel, but they are usually equipped to do so only as preparation for outreach events. In other words, the evangelistic training in most ministries is a tool for "cold call" evangelism done randomly on campus. Training students to live on mission amid a specific people group of students is much different. It is more like the training a missionary would get to learn to identify a people group, study the people group, live among the people group, demonstrate the gospel by blessing the people group, and find ways to contextualize the gospel message for the people group. Few, if any, campus ministries have this kind of training.

Campus ministers at UT made a commitment to campus saturation through missional communities back in 2002, but we never moved forward in a significant way until we partnered in equipping students through a course called the Retrospect Course. Glenn Smith, of New Church Initiatives, heard about what we were attempting at UT through his friend and ministry partner in Houston, Jim Herrington. Glenn had already been writing training material for students wanting to live like missionaries on campus. He took many of the same principles taught in his church planting courses and adapted them to the missional community movement at UT.

THIS CANNOT BE OVERSTATED: THE MEASURE OF GROWTH AND FRUIT IN THE MISSIONAL COMMUNITY MOVEMENT HAS A DIRECT PARALLEL TO THE DEPTH TO WHICH STUDENTS ARE EQUIPPED AND COACHED.

In 2003, we invited Glenn to train UT's missional community leaders, and about 40 students took the Retrospect Course. Over the following three years approximately 80 missional communities were trained to reach pockets of people on the UT campus. Many campus ministers who attended the course with their students were also equipped to teach students the material. After the third year of training, most of the ministers began teaching the same principles in their own unique ways to their students. Instead of outsourcing the training to Campus Renewal Ministries and New Church Initiatives, they began to own the vision and equip students themselves. It was then that the missional community movement really began to grow, as each ministry embraced the vision for itself and created its own training curriculum for missional community leaders.

Just as the ministries had to first change their thinking and then change their structures, students had to do the same. It was crucial to help students at UT shift their thinking from a "retreat mentality" to an "advancement mentality." We had to retrain their minds to believe God had sent them to UT on mission and that God could use them to transform their friends, instead of fearing that they would be defeated. When The Austin Stone Community Church caught the vision for missional communities, they launched an envisioning series of teachings that taught students, as well as their congregation, about the power of the gospel, God's heart for the lost, the believers' identities as missionaries, and the call of Jesus to go to the lost. Other ministries began to teach the same thing using their own terminology, and the movement really exploded. The vision casting from leaders in the large group setting was reinforced by equipping done in small group settings. Hill Country Bible Church UT changed their discipleship groups completely, making each adult leader not just an adult discipler, but a missionary coach, whose job included meeting weekly with students to collect reports from the mission field. The Texas Wesley United Methodist Campus Ministry formed a leadership team called the Outreach Council, whose only commitment to leadership within their ministry is to live on mission in an unbelieving community on campus. They meet weekly for coaching, prayer, and encouragement. This cannot be overstated: The measure of growth and fruit in the missional community movement has a direct parallel to the depth to which students are equipped and coached.

Campus Crusade has had tremendous impact on the Greek life at UT. Fraternities and sororities are reached with the gospel more than any other part of the UT campus. The Greek system is perfect for missional living due to the amount of time that Greeks spend together and because they raise up their own natural leadership from year to year. Crusade has tapped into the structure and lifestyle in such a way as to perpetually equip students to lead their missional communities year after year in dozens of the Greek houses. It has even resulted in equipping their future staff, since about 50 percent of Crusade staff at UT was once a part of a UT fraternity or sorority!

After years of participation, observation, and borrowing from many campus ministries' equipping components, last year CRM wrote our own training curriculum for missional communities (which we call Spark Groups). The course is called the Spark Course, and it is taught in person by CRM staff or online at www.campusrenewal.org. A video accompanies the course, documenting the stories of four students leading Spark Groups at UT, as they describe how they lived out each of the eight Spark Group practices. It teaches students how to put into action the eight practices of a Spark Group. We created the course so that other campuses who capture a vision for missional communities will not need to talk about doing it for years (like we did) before they get started equipping students. The Spark Course is simple, but profound. It is an easy way to get students on mission to specific people groups on your campus. Now, many UT campus ministries are using the course within their own ministries.

CRM's *Spark Course* is an eight-week course that equips students to start Spark Groups. *Students and campus ministers can take the Spark Course online or become Spark Course facilitators and order the Spark Course workbooks for their campus ministries. It teaches students to walk out the eight practices of Spark Groups.*

EIGHT SPARK GROUP PRACTICES

1. *Pick* a people group
Discern what people group God is calling to be your mission field.

2. *Partner* with other believers
Ask other believers to join you in mission.

3. *Pray* and plan
Pray every week, and ask the Lord to reveal His plans for you.

4. *Presence* in the community
Spend a significant amount of time each week in your community building relationships with many people.

5. *Prepare* **the way for the gospel**
Demonstrate the gospel to your community by being loving, living a holy life, and revealing the power of God.

6. *Proclaim* **the gospel**
Initiate spiritual conversations by asking questions, sharing your story, and sharing the gospel.

7. *Produce* **disciples**
Make disciples by meeting weekly to study the Bible, teaching your friends to obey the commands of Jesus.

8. *Reproduce* **Spark Groups**
Plant more Spark Groups by reproducing leaders and sending them to more unreached people groups.

Networking the Body

The movement expanded when we decentralized training and each campus ministry began to train its own missionaries instead of outsourcing them to CRM. However, in doing so we also lost something equally important: Networking. Every ministry began to train its own missional community leaders, but we never knew who was doing what among which people groups until the end of the year when I collected the year-end campus ministry survey. This created a huge problem because many ministries were attempting to reach the same communities but did not know it. Plus, on a college campus where turnover of leaders is so high, it is challenging to coordinate between ministries to keep missional communities going from one year to the next. If a student leader in a missional community involving several ministries graduated with no one ready to take his or her place, then we were not doing an adequate job of preparing new leaders. The root problem here is often one of poor networking.

The nature of missional communities is unique. They are formed from within a specific people group, rather than being part of a small group assimilation assignment. If a few students from Campus Crusade start a missional community in the Ultimate Frisbee club team at UT, odds are that students from other campus ministries are already a part of the team. Missional communities, more than anything else we do, require partnership with other ministries, because even when they start with a core team from one ministry, students from other ministries who are a part of that people group may join the missional community. Of the 220 missional communities at UT, 150 are joint efforts between campus ministries.

One of the more strategic departments for missional communities at UT is the nursing school. Students apply to get into the nursing school after their sophomore year. It's competitive and the class sizes are small. Those who get accepted into the program are in the same classes together for two years of nursing school, so they see each other almost every day. Knowing that this was a strategic department to reach, The Austin Stone Community Church, Hill Country Bible Church UT, and Campus Renewal Ministries each asked their nursing students to join together to form a missional community for their class. Heather, a staff person from Hill Country Bible Church, began meeting with the girls for coaching every few weeks, with the blessing of each ministry involved. Next year, CRM is taking over coaching this missional community, but students from many ministries will be a part of it.

> MISSIONAL COMMUNITIES, MORE THAN ANYTHING ELSE WE DO, REQUIRE PARTNERSHIP WITH OTHER MINISTRIES, BECAUSE EVEN WHEN THEY START WITH A CORE TEAM FROM ONE MINISTRY, STUDENTS FROM OTHER MINISTRIES WHO ARE A PART OF THAT PEOPLE GROUP MAY JOIN THE MISSIONAL COMMUNITY.

About a year ago (in 2009) we realized we needed to partner together more intentionally in order to see the campus saturated with missional communities. Ten ministries at UT stepped into a new partnership called Renovate UT. We agreed to meet monthly to report on our missional communities, once a semester for a united celebration, and to share a database of all of our missional community leaders so that we could know who was doing what where and how to connect students across ministry lines.

This was quite a commitment. It required a sacrifice of time just to add an extra monthly meeting, but more than that, it required a sacrifice of ownership. Nobody cared who received credit for any missional community. We just cared that one or two students took leadership and that the ministry most connected to those leaders was coaching them. If that was happening, then we asked all of our students who share a vision for the same community to join that group on mission.

As leaders graduate, students from other ministries may take over leadership, in which case their campus ministers assume the coaching responsibility for that missional community. It's completely radical to share like this! We are able to do this because our vision is to reach every student, not to grow our individual ministries. We are hoping someday, by God's grace, to disciple the whole campus.

Partnership is vital. Missional communities, by nature, involve students from many ministries who live in the same place, hang out together, enjoy the same activities, are in the same classes, and are called to the same people. One ministry can begin to send students out as missionaries, but a campus can never be saturated until ministries are in relationship with one another, sharing conversation, information, resources, and even sharing students!

" What if the goal of the different campus ministries was not to get more Christian students "in" their respective organizations, but instead to get more Christian students "out" among the culture of the campus? What if campus ministries agreed that helping students grow in their faith should take place in the everyday situations and relationships of those students? What if Christian students were encouraged to be salt and light in the places where

God already has them living and doing life?

For these things to be true, campus ministries would have to care as much about the whole campus as they do about the success of their own groups. By God's grace, this is what is happening at the University of Texas! A coalition of campus ministries is working together to help students live out their faith in areas all over campus. And in doing so, we are attempting to connect Christian students with each other rather than keeping them separated in our own ministry affiliations.

As an example, I've seen students from several different ministries who are architecture students working together to bless that college. They pray together regularly, they move toward their peers in love, and they seek to live out the gospel. Similarly, our ministry (Campus Crusade for Christ) has students who are resident assistants in a large all-female dorm. We encourage them to work alongside students from other ministries who live in that dorm, so that together they can share the love of Christ there. This same thing is happening in fraternities, clubs, and living areas all over campus. There is genuine freedom in this, because it relieves the pressure of trying to build our own little kingdoms and allows us to focus on building and extending God's big Kingdom at UT. 🔒🔒

TODD STEWMAN
Campus Crusade for Christ
CAMPUS MINISTER, 2003–2010

Marketplace and Missions

Recently, I was able to spend a week in Ethiopia with my wife Brenda and her family. She and her three brothers grew up there, while her dad worked as a professor of agricultural engineering. It was a sentimental journey, as we remembered Brenda's father, who loved the Ethiopian people and who went to be with the Lord about a year before the trip.

One day while I was there I was able to meet up with Courtney Tardy, a 2008 UT graduate who is doing mission work among the Somali people in eastern Ethiopia. When Courtney was a student at UT, she was the first to lead a missional community to Muslim students. I would always see her on campus with African and Middle Eastern students that she had befriended. Now here I was halfway across the world sitting with her in a small living room having Somali tea and watching the World Cup with her new friends.

I asked her how her time at UT prepared her for what she is now doing. She said her heart for missions and for Africa grew at UT in large part because of the emphasis her campus ministry placed on living on mission. While she said she had to learn a lot more about the culture and language, she said she did not need to learn how to be a missionary. She had been living as a missionary years before she arrived in Africa.

I once heard Bill Bright say, "Change the campus and you change the world." He was right. What if college students learn to live as missionaries on campus where they live, work, and play? If so, they will live on mission in our cities and around the world where they live, work, and play. International students, those who take jobs abroad, and those who take jobs in our country would not need to be equipped to be missionaries. It would be second nature to be a missionary in the marketplace or in communities overseas.

Those who have led missional communities at the nursing school will easily live on mission at their hospitals. Those who have led missional communities on the track team will do so in the running communities in their cities. Those who have led missional communities in the apartment complexes will continue to do so in their apartment buildings and homes after college. Even those who have been called to traditional missions overseas will be equipped. They will know how to engage and interpret culture, build relationships, love and serve people, contextualize the gospel to their communities, and disciple their friends who want to follow Jesus with them. The hope for cities and nations is our students, if only we can equip them to be missionaries while they are on our campuses.

" The day that I walked past 21st St. Co-op and heard Daft Punk pumping out of the kitchen windows was the day that I knew that I would have future encounters with the co-op world. Cooperative living is best described as an alternative college student housing option involving eating, laboring, and communing with your fellow housemates.

Some co-ops are very familial and tame. 21st St. Co-op is notorious for being wild, abandoning social norms, and knowing how to truly "live it up." In the summer of 2007, I decided to tractor-beam my missional focus on this 100-person hippie village and, by the will and direction of the Lord, share Christ with those I met. I started by finding a Jesus-loving team that lived in the co-op to join me.

After that, about once every two months, we started putting on Open Mic Nights in the co-op's music venue to serve the students by helping them display their talent in a familiar, but structured environment. After we started building friendships, we naturally began having spiritual conversations. Ultimately, dozens of students began to join us weekly for Bible discussions at the co-op. We were able to have meaningful conversations about Jesus Christ with people who would never attend church. By serving the community first, we showed them that we cared about their lives before we shared our faith with them.

The year and a half that I invested in the co-op humbled me and showed me that God knows how to reach people's hearts better than I do. Now my missionary life is continually being shaped by how well I listen to people and translate what they say about their culture by loving them with my words and lifestyle. "

SARAH TOOLEY
Hill Country Bible Church UT
UT GRADUATE, 2008

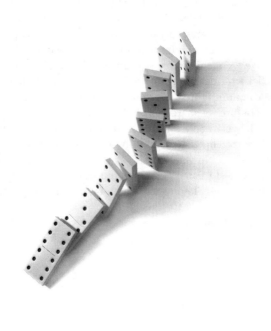

CATALYTIC
events

> **COLLABORATIVE INITIATIVES THAT ACCELERATE AND SUSTAIN GOD'S REVEALED PLAN FOR CAMPUS TRANSFORMATION.**

My senior year at UT (1995) I met a student named Jeremy Story. Jeremy had pulled together students from several different ministries to plan the first "Resurrection Week" (aka Rez Week). We realized that our vision was similar, so we began to work together. Ironically, many of the students working with him for Rez Week were involved in ministries not represented in our weekly united prayer gathering. So when we began working together, nearly 100 percent of the campus ministries were represented. We continued to meet weekly for prayer and planning.

Almost every campus ministry agreed to cancel their regular worship gatherings in order to come together as one united Body during Holy Week. Hundreds of students participated in that first Rez Week, which started with a concert of prayer and turned into a night of open mic confession lasting so long that we were literally kicked out of the lecture hall when the janitor had to lock the doors. Rez Week continued with several nights of united worship and an evangelistic message where dozens indicated decisions for Christ. It was an amazing week, led by a team of students representing nearly every campus ministry at UT. The event itself was a huge success. It was a great symbol of the unity that was developing between ministries as students were meeting together in prayer. Rez Week even led to more students joining our weekly united prayer group, which was fantastic. We were thrilled with what God did during that week, so much so that we immediately began planning the next Rez Week.

After that first Rez Week, there was such a hunger among students to work together as one Body of Christ that it became a full-time job to lead the movement. I graduated and started raising funds through a non-profit that a number of pastors in Austin had established for start-up ministries like ours. Two years later, Jeremy graduated and established Campus Renewal Ministries as its own non-profit. I remained at UT, leading the movement there, while Jeremy developed Campus Renewal Ministries nationally.

One of the first things he did was write a Rez Week manual to help students on other campuses organize their own Rez Week events. At one time we had more than 100 campuses doing Rez Week together. For several years we even linked the campuses via satellite during one of the nights of Rez Week. In 1998, UT was the first campus to host the satellite broadcast. Rez Week has continued to be a yearly event at UT and on many other campuses to this day.

As great as Rez Week was at UT and on other campuses, Jeremy and I kept wrestling with the age-old question when it comes to campus ministry events: "What is the real impact?" Every campus ministry wrestles with this question. Events take so much energy, manpower, and money. You constantly have to weigh the cost versus the benefits. Is it going to make a lasting impact? Is it going to move students deeper into community and leadership? Perhaps most important, is it going to move students into the more strategic parts of your campus ministry? If these questions need to be asked by individual ministries when it comes to their own events, then they need to be asked even louder when it comes to unified events. Jeremy and I found ourselves asking, "Does Rez Week move students into missional communities? Does it grow the prayer movement? Does it help develop a spiritual map? Does it result in more students and ministers participating in the Fusion Group? We needed Rez Week to move us further along in the campus-reaching vision. We did not need an event. We needed a catalytic event.

The first few years, Rez Week was not a catalytic event, primarily because the campus ministers and students were just beginning to pray together. After a few years of prayer, however, relationships and vision began to grow, and we began to partner in more long-term, strategic ways. As we made commitments to mobilize prayer, spiritually map the campus, and build missional communities, we started asking, "How can we use Rez Week and other united events to move our students and ministries in these directions?"

I distinctly remember Rez Week in 2001. We had just made a commitment to mobilize prayer together, to try to build the type of prayer movement that normally precedes revival. That Rez Week we decided to do our first season of 24/7 prayer. We pitched a tent in the middle of campus and had students from all of our ministries sign up to lead an hour of worship and prayer, one after another, 24 hours a day. Students loved it and really sought God that week. The tent was the most crowded from midnight to 4 A.M. (so I am told). In the evenings, we united for worship and teaching on the topic of prayer. We even invited some of the folks from the International House of Prayer in Kansas City to teach and lead us. Guess what happened? The prayer movement grew that year. It was a catalytic event.

As I already mentioned, after our first survey of the Christian community at UT, we were very disturbed by the fact that 34 percent of men in our ministries said they looked at pornography once a week or more. During the Rez Week following that survey of the Christian community in 2002, we held an event called the "Power of Porn." A male and female speaker spoke for two nights on the topic of pornography, its tragic effects on their lives, and the freedom they found in Christ. It was a powerful Rez Week, well thought out and purposely planned. It was a springboard for confession and discipleship related to these significant issues facing almost every one of our students. It was a catalytic event.

Biblical Basis for Catalytic Events

Calendared Catalytic Events

We cannot grow in the Lord apart from developing our personal relationship with God by studying scripture and seeking Him through prayer. It is equally vital to our spiritual growth to be committed to a number of relationships in a local fellowship where we can worship, pray, and study the scripture together. While these are the primary means for developing our walk with Jesus, there is also a place for catalytic events. These events are less frequent than our personal time with God and our worship together in smaller communities, but they often have a greater impact, and they are used by God to move us closer to Him and closer to community. Most of us can point to some catalytic event that changed our lives. God would not ask us to gather for catalytic events if He did not recognize the life-changing power of such experiences.

"Three times a year all your men must appear before the LORD your God at the place he will choose: at the Feast of Unleavened Bread, the Feast of Weeks, and the Feast of Tabernacles. No man should appear before the LORD empty-handed: Each of you must bring a gift in proportion to the way the LORD your God has blessed you" (Deuteronomy 16:16–17).

God asked the 12 tribes of Israel to unite three times a year. He knew that they could not possibly meet together all the time, that even once a month would be too much. Still, God thought it was important enough to meet together that He asked every tribe to travel from distant lands to a place that He chose so that they could worship together three times a year (and not without lugging some gifts along the way!).

I am not suggesting that the same is required for us (to have three united gatherings a year), but I am saying that it is God's heart for His people to unite regularly. If He wanted Israel to sacrifice in such a dramatic way several times a year, certainly He would like us to do the same. The sacrifice we need to make to meet together is not comparable with the sacrifice they made in order to meet together three times a year. It's not unlike the need for denominations and national campus ministries to have their annual conventions. Organizations simply need a time or two a year to be together in worship, to be reminded of the vision, to share stories of what God is doing, and to get on the same page.

MOST OF US CAN POINT TO SOME CATALYTIC EVENT THAT CHANGED OUR LIVES. GOD WOULD NOT ASK US TO GATHER FOR CATALYTIC EVENTS IF HE DID NOT RECOGNIZE THE LIFE-CHANGING POWER OF SUCH EXPERIENCES.

At UT, we have several regular united gatherings. We have Rez Week on the last week of March every year. We have All Campus Worship and the Campus Minister Luncheon the first

Thursday of October that does not conflict with the Texas/OU football weekend (you plan the fall semester around football at Texas!). In addition, the ministries that are part of Renovate UT have a once a semester united celebration to share missional community stories while eating barbecue. Most ministries at UT have these dates written in their calendars as if they were their own events. It gives us enough needed time together, but not too much so as to take us away from the fruitful work we are doing as individual ministries.

Spontaneous Catalytic Events

Catalytic events in the Bible were not limited to three times a year. Throughout scripture there are many times when God called His people together for a specific purpose. Consider Elijah, in I Kings 18, when he called all Israel and the prophets of Baal together for a showdown on Mount Carmel. I would call that a catalytic event! At the end of the day, everyone "fell prostrate and cried, 'The LORD — He is God! The LORD — He is God!'" (I Kings 18:39). Consider Samuel when he said, "'Assemble all Israel at Mizpah and I will intercede with the LORD for you'" (I Samuel 7:5). Everyone gathered, and it turned into a time of united fasting and repentance. God heard their prayers and turned back the Philistines, who were attacking them. In Nehemiah 9, all of Israel gathered for a time of worship and repentance. They read the law for a quarter of the day and then spent another quarter of the day in worship and confession. At the end of the day they wrote a covenant of purity to the Lord, and all of the spiritual leaders sealed the covenant together. Paul, in Acts 19, had an old-fashioned revival where people came forward to throw their idolatrous possessions into a fire. Everything that was burned totaled 50,000 days' wages!

These stories, and many more, are examples of additional catalytic events — events planned by leaders in response to a specific situation facing them. As leaders on campus begin to pray together, to spiritually map the campus, and to mobilize missional communities, God will lead them to many different catalytic events that will help advance their long-term, strategic initiatives. There will be seasons when they know they are called to unite the Body of Christ for a specific purpose. When they do, they will be echoing the voice of Joel when he said, "Blow the trumpet in Zion, declare a holy fast, call a sacred assembly. Gather the people, consecrate the assembly; bring together the elders, gather the children, those nursing at the breast. Let the bridegroom leave his room and the bride her chamber. Let the priests, who minister before the LORD, weep between the porch and the altar. Let them say, 'Spare your people, O LORD. Do not make your inheritance an object of scorn, a byword among the nations. Why should they say among the peoples, 'Where is their God?'" (Joel 2:15–17). There are times when the whole Body of Christ on campus needs to gather for a time of repentance, a time of vision casting, a time of teaching, or an evangelistic outreach. It's biblical to do so.

THERE ARE TIMES WHEN THE WHOLE BODY OF CHRIST ON CAMPUS NEEDS TO GATHER FOR A TIME OF REPENTANCE, A TIME OF VISION CASTING, A TIME OF TEACHING, OR AN EVANGELISTIC OUTREACH. IT'S BIBLICAL TO DO SO.

There was a time when we as ministers believed in the campus-reaching vision, but we were not sure our students were catching the full vision. We started talking about the idea of doing some united vision casting for a season. We felt like God was in it, so we moved forward, planning a campaign we called "The CAUSE." For five weeks, 16 ministries committed to teach on the CAUSE topics (Character, Asking (prayer), Unity, Service, Evangelism). We created some great videos that introduced the topic for the week and communicated that this was a campus-wide message. Our only commitment was to use the videos and teach on the specific topic. Each ministry could use any scripture to teach the topic. It ended up that many of the 16 ministries did "pulpit swaps" during the five weeks, which really helped communicate that this was a campus-wide vision. Imagine if you could identify some problem through spiritual mapping and all agree to teach on the topic for weeks at a time. Talk about a united voice!

Important Pointers in Planning Catalytic Events

Not Too Many

It's important, when it comes to catalytic events, to have just enough, but not too many. The campus is not going to be reached if we continue to meet together all of the time. Students need to be on campus, living on mission in their communities. Ministers need to be discipling students and developing strategies. The campus can only be reached when we are all doing our specific roles, as individual students and as individual ministries. The secret to catalytic events is finding the right time to call students together so that students' and campus ministries' efforts are enhanced, not distracted. Ministries need their own catalytic events to build community and cast vision, just as the whole Body of Christ needs these events. You have to choose one or two events to champion each semester, and that's about it. So you must choose carefully.

> **THE CAMPUS CAN ONLY BE REACHED WHEN WE ARE ALL DOING OUR SPECIFIC ROLES, AS INDIVIDUAL STUDENTS AND AS INDIVIDUAL MINISTRIES. THE SECRET TO CATALYTIC EVENTS IS FINDING THE RIGHT TIME TO CALL STUDENTS TOGETHER SO THAT STUDENTS' AND CAMPUS MINISTRIES' EFFORTS ARE ENHANCED, NOT DISTRACTED.**

When it comes to united catalytic events, it is helpful to have one each semester that is constant. For us it is All Campus Worship in the fall and Rez Week in the spring. Everyone plans around these events, and we keep them the same time each year. Then you can just spend time in prayer and conversation about what you want the focus of this year's event to be. Any additional events that spring up from your times of prayer and planning can be secondary events, when only those who are able participate.

Not for Everyone

We've said it is important to have one event each semester where the whole Body of Christ comes together. It is also beneficial to have events in which just three or four of the ministries participate. In 2010, Campus Crusade took the lead on an outreach event called "Girls Night Out." Several of the ministries canceled their events in order to participate, while others had their large group meetings on the same night just like they did every week. Some of the ministries who met on different nights than the event really promoted it, encouraging their students to take part. Others, not wanting to ask their students to do one more thing, chose not to promote the event at all. No matter how the ministries chose to participate, we still came together the next week for united prayer, heard testimonies of what God did that night, and rejoiced together.

Often there are secondary events that some ministries collaborate on and some do not. The key is knowing the difference between secondary events and united events and clearly communicating the expectations for each so that no one is disappointed. It also happens that some ministries, depending on circumstances, cannot participate in the united events. There is no judgment there either. The posture needs to be such that every campus ministry can choose their own level of involvement in catalytic events without feeling like they are not a part of the movement if they are less committed to a particular event. This is why praying together each week is so important.

For instance, during the summer of 2010, 11 campus ministries united to have a weekly time of worship, teaching, and fellowship. Since so many ministers are in and out of town during the summer, we thought it would be good to combine our efforts to lessen the burden on individual ministries to plan something excellent every week. We offered every ministry the opportunity to be a part of the united worship. Some preferred to emphasize their own weekly gatherings in order to build their specific communities during the summer. They were free to say that they preferred to do their own thing during the summer, and none of the 11 participating ministries were bothered by their decision. When ministries want to partner for a specific

THE POSTURE NEEDS TO BE SUCH THAT EVERY CAMPUS MINISTRY CAN CHOOSE THEIR OWN LEVEL OF INVOLVEMENT IN CATALYTIC EVENTS WITHOUT FEELING LIKE THEY ARE NOT A PART OF THE MOVEMENT IF THEY ARE LESS COMMITTED TO A PARTICULAR EVENT.

event, an invitation is extended to everyone. Those who wish to participate can add it to their calendar and be part of the leadership while those who do not want to participate can bless the event and choose not to promote it within their ministries.

Outside Voices

One way to be sure an event is a catalytic one is to bring the right people to speak at the event. If the aim of the event is to mobilize prayer, then bring in an excellent communicator who is passionate about prayer. If you want the event to mobilize missional communities, then bring in an excellent communicator who is passionate about missional communities. As fun as it may sound to plan an event where campus ministers share the teaching and vision casting, we have found that an outside voice is received even better.

In 2003, we were trying to help ministers and students catch a vision for transformation. We hoped that at the end of Rez Week they would believe that God is able to radically transform

UT, and we wanted them to understand some of the biblical prerequisites to revival. That year we brought in Jackson Senyonga as our guest speaker. Jackson was one of the many pastors who had been uniting in prayer and mission in Uganda. He was on the stage on December 31, 1999, when the Ugandan people held an all-night prayer and worship gathering at their soccer stadium to officially dedicate the nation of Uganda to God for the next century. Talk about an outside voice! Something really changed in the campus ministers after he met with about 20 of us and told how he and other leaders tithe their time to the city, giving 10 percent of their workweek to ministry outside of their churches. Suddenly praying together once a week seemed rather simple, and the attendance at campus minister prayer almost doubled.

In 2007, we were focusing on calling students to mission on campus. We wanted to see the missional community movement grow. We planned to use Rez Week to challenge students to commit to leading missional communities for the following year. That spring we invited Neil Cole, author of *Organic Church*, and Jaeson Ma, author of *The Blueprint*, to come to Rez Week. God used their outside voices and incredible testimonies to inspire students to stop huddling in their Christian communities and to live on mission in a specific community on campus. Two hundred students responded to the message, and about 100 new missional communities were birthed that spring semester. Incredibly, 60 of the missional communities survived the initial wave of emotional commitments and continued into the fall. God used that Rez Week to bring the missional community movement to the forefront of our work together.

The right voice is always important. *City Reaching*, the book campus ministers read together, recommended having someone from the outside to help get the conversation about city reaching started among leaders. That is why we asked Jim Herrington to meet with us. We needed someone from the outside to lead us in conversation. We needed someone without an agenda, other than to help us discover God's purposes for us together. It was invaluable. Campus Renewal Ministries offers our services to this end as well. When a student or minister from another campus shares our vision and gathers others to hear from CRM staff about the story of UT and other campuses where we are working, we almost always see a campus minister or student leader Fusion Group started after we leave. CRM staff is available to be that outside voice for you.

    As a freshman at UT, I attended my first Rez Week in March 2007. Although this event was almost four years ago, I still consider it a time when my life was changed, and my relationship with Jesus was radically impacted.

I still remember hearing Jaeson Ma preach on the Great Commission and talk about what it meant to live out our faith in what he called "missional communities." Although I had been a Christian since middle school, this was the first time I had heard the Great Commission and the idea that I could be a missionary even now, as I was going to school at UT.

I'm not sure what my four years at UT would have looked like if I hadn't heard that exact message at that exact time in my life. Through the speakers that week, a vision was instilled in me that still exists to this day. God gave me the revelation that my faith wasn't just about me and my Christian bubble. I realized that God's purpose was much larger than me, and that He wanted me to be a part of it.

The last night of Rez Week, I committed to living out a missional lifestyle in a specific community on the UT campus, and I watched many of my friends and peers do the same. This was definitely a new and exciting commitment in my faith, but it made a lasting impact on the remainder of my time at UT. For the rest of my college career, I led a missional community in the nursing school and I learned what it looks like to live missionally on a day-to-day basis.

Erin Chandler
Campus Renewal Ministries
UT Graduate, 2010

Corporate Vision and Community

Every year I ask our student leadership team, "What would you guys think about canceling Rez Week this year?" I don't ask it sarcastically. I really am willing to scrap it, if it is time to do so. Every year that I ask, however, I get a dramatic response: "What? Are you crazy?" Students go on to say how much they love Rez Week — that it is their favorite week of the year. There is nothing like that one week to bring the whole Body of Christ together, to serve together with new friends from different ministries and hear the same message throughout the week. We're on campus together 24 hours a day. There is no substitute for the community and vision that are built up during Rez Week.

CATALYTIC EVENTS MOVE STUDENTS AND MINISTERS FURTHER ALONG IN THE CAMPUS-REACHING STRATEGIES, BUT THEY ALSO SERVE ANOTHER COMMUNAL PURPOSE. THEY ARE A PLACE TO CAST CORPORATE VISION AND A PLACE TO BUILD CORPORATE COMMUNITY.

Catalytic events move students and ministers further along in the campus-reaching strategies, but they also serve another communal purpose. They are a place to cast corporate vision and a place to build corporate community. United events can be used to clearly present what God is doing on campus and what the specific next steps are for the Body of Christ. Students and ministers leave an event with greater clarity about exactly what God is doing on campus and what part they have to play. Since there is a turnover of students and ministers every year, events are necessary for casting a clear vision.

Additionally, catalytic events have value in that they develop a greater sense of corporate community. Simply being in the same vicinity makes a difference. After a significant catalytic event, students and ministers get the sense that they are a part of something bigger, which of course they are. There is tremendous value in simply being together, hearing stories from one another, and praying with one another. It helps give you a sense that you are just a small part of the whole, and that is beautiful. Catalytic events give you the opportunity to see that you are not alone and that God is really moving on campus.

> As a senior in high school, I expected to be accepted into a school other than UT. When I realized I was not accepted, I was, honestly, a little bitter. Just before graduation, I decided to visit the UT campus during Rez Week, to see what the Christian community was like there. I did not want to like anything about UT, but I went hoping God would give me a small glimpse of my future at UT.
>
> My attitude dramatically changed that night when I walked up to Gregory Gym where Rez Week took place. I felt the Holy Spirit moving in me. Little things were just shaking up my world. God used the art panels, the speaker, the worship time, and the people to shake that bitterness away from me. What I saw that night made me want to be part of God's work at UT. God was moving in that group of believers and I knew I wanted to be part of it.
>
> The next year, God allowed me the joy of joining the student Fusion Group and helping plan Rez Week. I did not realize the unity required to pull off such a huge event. There were students from all different ministries, majors, and ethnicities, but all were united with one dream: to see Christ glorified on the campus of UT.
>
> Rez Week would never work if just one ministry attempted it. It requires all the ministries to work in partnership. God uses Rez Week to give the Body of Christ a greater sense of community by allowing strangers to work together, sing together, pray together, and serve together. I thank God every day for allowing me to see the beauty of Rez Week during my senior year of high school and totally changing my opinion of the spiritual climate of UT. If it were not for Rez Week, I honestly do not know if I would have allowed God to use me my freshman year.

TANISHA BUSH
The Austin Stone Community Church
UT STUDENT, CLASS OF 2013

CONCLUSION: Beyond Campus

I will be the first to tell you that we are not there yet. For 19 years we have been praying for revival, asking God to bring the type of transformation that has happened on campuses throughout history and is happening in cities and nations around the world today. We certainly have not seen transformation. Our most grand, faith-filled prayers remain unanswered so far. I like to think that God has a saved folder in His inbox where He is collecting our many prayers for a historic revival at UT. I believe one day it will be His time, and revival will come to our campus. The good news is, when He does bring the harvest, we will be ready and able to disciple the whole campus. While we've yet to see the harvest, we are more and more prepared.

At a conference in Austin, I remember hearing Ed Silvoso from Harvest Evangelism say, "What if half of your city put their faith in Jesus. Would you be ready to disciple them?" In a few years, we hope to be able to say "yes" to that question. Some day we want to have believers living on mission in every college, club, residence, and culture at UT. Our goal is to have believers in relationship with literally all 50,000 students at UT, so that if God brought the harvest, we would be ready. This, however, is just one way of measuring how prepared we are for transformation, and it is less significant than the more important preparation that is taking place in the hearts of believers at UT.

II Chronicles 7:14 says, "If my people who are called by my name will humble themselves and pray, and seek my face, and turn from their wicked ways, then I will hear from heaven, forgive their sin, and heal their land." Here is where the real stage is being set for an outpouring of the Holy Spirit on campus. It is measured by the growing humility we have toward one another in the Body of Christ, by the way we are uniting to pray over 100 hours a week, and by the way we are addressing sin and strongholds on campus and in the Christian community. This is the spiritual work that prepares a campus for God's presence. This is the scripture we hold on to and pray into, believing God will do what He promised as we continue to seek Him together.

City Reaching

Just last week I sat in a meeting with more than 300 pastors in Austin. It was a historic meeting. They gathered to hear data and have conversation about what was discovered through Austin's first city-wide spiritual mapping campaign. At the end of the evening, a number of pastors cast a vision for what it would look like for churches in Austin to work together to reach every resident with the gospel of Jesus and meet every need of the city, specifically education, housing, and health care. Several leading pastors had been meeting for months before this gathering. They freed up their schedules to be together for hours each week to pray and talk about ways to reach the city together. They made an agreement to tithe their time to the city, spending 10 percent of their week working together and praying to develop a city-wide vision that was outside of the scope of their individual fellowships. At the gathering, they asked other pastors to begin to do the same. As amazing at that sounds, it is really becoming the norm. Gatherings like this are taking place in cities all around the world, as the Body of Christ is being awakened to the need to work together to reach cities with the gospel of Jesus.

Truthfully, I get overwhelmed when I think of city reaching. A campus of 50,000 where ministers are in much greater proximity seems so much more doable. I believe, however, that what God is doing at UT can be duplicated in our cities, especially if we are sending students out into the marketplace and into churches where they already know how live on mission and work with their brothers and sisters from other churches to demonstrate and declare the gospel where they live, work, and play. Plus, many college pastors later become senior pastors and leaders of the church in the city. If they, too, have the campus-reaching DNA, then they will become leaders in the city-reaching movement, mobilizing their congregations to do the same.

What the believers have experienced at the University of Texas in working as one Body to reach the whole campus can inform the way they live out their faith and participate in Christian community in Austin and around the world. We are helping shape a new type of Christian at UT — one who believes God can transform cities, one who prays diligently for God to do something great in a city, one who believes there is one Body of Christ in the city and humbly unites in mission with believers in his or her neighborhood and marketplace. These are the type of Christians who will witness our cities being transformed.

Beyond UT

Texas graduates scatter around the state, the country, and the world. A degree from UT does open doors for you. As difficult as it is to have hundreds of believers graduate every year, there is a strategic benefit to campus ministry. Campus ministry works more like a missions-sending agency. Every year we send hundreds of missionaries out into the marketplace, to cities and countries around the world. Those who leave our campuses will be the next generation of teachers, politicians, lawyers, pastors, entrepreneurs, musicians, social workers, nurses, doctors, missionaries, artists, and parents. That is a major reason why we are in campus ministry. That is why so many of you reading this book have given your lives to college ministry. You believe that the four or five years you are privileged to have with students will help shape a new generation of Christian leaders who integrate their faith in the marketplace and neighborhoods throughout our cities and around the world. We believe this too. We believe UT's slogan to be true — and prophetic: "What starts here changes the world."

ABOUT CAMPUS RENEWAL MINISTRIES

Campus Renewal Ministries (CRM) was founded at the University of Texas and is headquartered on the UT campus in Austin, Texas. CRM has staff and volunteers on many campuses and consults and provides resources for students and campus ministers across the country.

Contact us at www.campusrenewal.org or at:

Campus Renewal Ministries
2421 #B San Antonio St.
Austin, TX 78705
(512) 331-5991

CRM Vision

Campus Renewal Ministries forges partnerships in prayer to build missional communities that transform college campuses with the gospel of Jesus.

CRM Ventures

Fusion Groups

Campus ministers and/or student leaders who pray together weekly with other leaders to grow in relationship and to partner in mission for the transformation of their campus.

> *"I want men everywhere to lift up holy hands in prayer, without anger or disputing" (I Timothy 2:8).*

Spark Groups

Groups of students united in prayer and mission to demonstrate and to declare the gospel of Jesus and to make disciples from within a specific people group on campus.

"As you sent me into the world, I have sent them into the world" (John 17:18).

Prayer Movements

Mobilizing campus ministers and students to seek God for the transformation of the campus through fasting and prayer.

"After they prayed, the place where they were meeting was shaken. And they were all filled with the Holy Spirit and spoke the word of God boldly" (Acts 4:31).

Catalytic Events

Collaborating on initiatives that accelerate and build into the campus-reaching movement.

"Three times a year all your men must appear before the LORD your God at the place he will choose: at the Feast of Unleavened Bread, the Feast of Weeks and the Feast of Tabernacles. No man should appear before the LORD empty-handed..." (Deuteronomy 16:16).

Spiritual Mapping

Systematic gathering and evaluation of data through surveys, research, and spiritual perceptions in order to discover the factors, influences, and trends that deter or advance God's work on campuses.

"Then I said to them, 'You see the trouble we are in: Jerusalem lies in ruins, and its gates have been burned with fire. Come, let us rebuild the wall of Jerusalem, and we will no longer be in disgrace'" (Nehemiah 2:17).

CRM Values

Christ Centered

Jesus is the head of the Church. We unite to exalt Him, to seek Him, and to make Him known.

> *"And he is the head of the body, the church; he is the beginning and the firstborn from among the dead, so that in everything he might have the supremacy" (Colossians 1:18).*

Transformation Focused

God's vision to transform college campuses is bigger than any one ministry. We partner in mission to see God's glory known on campus and beyond.

> *"For the earth will be filled with the knowledge of the glory of the Lord, as the waters cover the sea" (Habakkuk 2:14).*

Relationship Driven

The depth of our relationships must match the breadth of our vision for transformation. We value one another and need one another. We humble ourselves before one another, consider each other better than ourselves, and look to others' interests above our own.

> *"Do nothing out of selfish ambition or vain conceit, but in humility consider others better than yourselves. Each of you should look not only to your own interests, but also to the interests of others" (Philippians 2:3–4).*

Presence Propelled

Campus transformation begins by inviting God's presence to the campus. We need God's presence on our campus to see it transformed, so we pray and wait for God to do the work.

> *"For we do not preach ourselves, but Jesus Christ as Lord, and ourselves as your servants for Jesus's sake. For God, who said, 'Let light shine out of darkness,' made his light shine in our hearts to give us the light of the knowledge of the glory of God in the face of Christ" (II Corinthians 4:5–6).*

Purity Prescripted

God will not bring transformation until the Body of Christ repents from its sins. We seek holiness, love, humility, character, and personal transformation.

> *"...if my people, who are called by my name, will humble themselves and pray and seek my face and turn from their wicked ways, then will I hear from heaven and will forgive their sin and will heal their land" (II Chronicles 7:14).*

Mission Directed

Mission will always flow out of Christ-centered, transformation-focused relationships and prayer. As we pray together asking God for transformation, we also listen for and obey the Holy Spirit's direction toward collaborative mission.

> *"While they were worshiping the Lord and fasting, the Holy Spirit said, 'Set apart for me Barnabas and Saul for the work to which I have called them.' So after they had fasted and prayed, they placed their hands on them and sent them off" (Acts 13:2–3).*

ABOUT THE AUTHOR

Justin Christopher is the director of Campus Renewal Ministries (CRM) at the University of Texas. He helped start CRM as a student at UT from 1991 to 1995 and graduated with a Bachelor of Science in Speech Communications. He has worked for CRM since 1995, giving leadership to one of the most unique campus-reaching efforts of our generation. Justin is a true "orange-blood" and has devoted his life to seeing UT transformed by the gospel of Jesus. Justin and his wife Brenda live in Austin, Texas, and share their home with Leon, their black cat, and Lou, their 220-pound English Mastiff.